FILLETS OF PLAICE

GERALD DURRELL

Fillets of Plaice

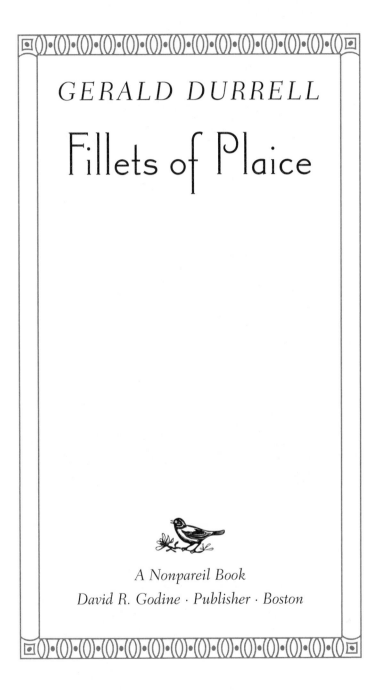

A Nonpareil Book
David R. Godine · Publisher · Boston

This is a Nonpareil Book
published in 2008 by
DAVID R. GODINE, *Publisher*
Post Office Box 450
Jaffrey, New Hampshire 03452
www.godine.com

LIBRARY OF CONGRESS CATALOGING-IN-PUBLICATION DATA

Durrell, Gerald, 1925–1995.
Fillets of plaice / Gerald Durrell.
p.   cm.
ISBN-13: 978-1-56792-354-4
ISBN-10: 1-56792-354-2
1. Durrell, Gerald, 1925–1995.
2. Durrell, Gerald, 1925–1995—Family.
3. Natural history—Greece—Corfu Island.
4. Corfu Island (Greece)—Description and travel.
I. Title.
PR6054.U74Z5 2008
828'.9'1403—dc22
[B]
2007050529

SECOND PRINTING, 2016
Printed in the United States of America

❊ Contents ❊

This book is for my brother Larry, who has always encouraged me to write and has rejoiced more than anyone in what success I have had.

"The child is mad, snails in his pockets!"
Lawrence Durrell, circa 1931

"The child is mad, scorpions in matchboxes!"
Lawrence Durrell, circa 1935

"The boy is mad, working in a pet shop!"
Lawrence Durrell, circa 1939

"The boy is mad, wanting to be a zoo keeper!"
Lawrence Durrell, circa 1945

"The man is mad, crawling about snake-infested jungles!"
Lawrence Durrell, circa 1952

"The man is mad, wanting to have a zoo!"
Lawrence Durrell, circa 1958

"The man is mad. Invite him to stay and he puts an eagle in your wine cellar!"
Lawrence Durrell, circa 1967

"The man is mad."
Lawrence Durrell, circa 1971

❀ The Birth of a Title ❀

THE DAY WAS one of those breathless, clear, blue days that only Greece, of all countries in the world, can provide. The cicadas were zithering in the olive trees and the sea was a deeper blue, moving reflection of the sky. We had just finished a large and leisurely lunch under the twisted, pitted olives that grew almost down to the edge of the sea on one of the most beautiful beaches in Corfu. The female members of the party had gone down to bathe and left Larry and myself alone. We slouched there indolently, thoughtfully ferrying a giant, wicker-covered bottle of turpentine-like retsina between us. We drank and mused in silence. Anyone who thinks that when authors meet they indulge in witty exchanges and saucy badinage is sadly mistaken.

"This is a nice retsina," said Larry at last, thoughtfully filling his glass. "Where did you get it?"

"From a little man who has a shop in one of those alleyways leading off Saint Spiridion Square. It is nice, isn't it?"

"Very," said Larry, holding the glass up to the light so that it glowed a very pale old gold. "The last bottle I got from town tasted and looked like a urine sample from a mule. It probably was."

"I'm coming this way tomorrow," I said. "I'll bring you a flagon if you like."

"Hmmm," said Larry. "Bring me a couple."

Exhausted by the intellectual exchange, we filled our glasses and lapsed into silence again. The ants were foraging over the remains of our food. Tiny, black, busy ones, large, leggy, red ones, with their behinds cocked up like anti-aircraft guns. On the bark of the olive against which I was leaning there were flocks of curious larvæ moving. Minute, fluffy creatures that looked like misshapen and rather dirty polar bears.

"What are you working on now?" Larry inquired.

I looked at him in surprise. We had an unspoken and unwritten law that we never discussed what we called Our Art with each other, lest it lead to dissension and vulgar abuse.

"I'm not working on anything at the moment, but I've got a sort of vague idea of something. As a matter of fact, I got the idea from reading *Spirit of Place*."

Larry snorted derisively. *Spirit of Place* was a compilation of his letters to his friends, painstakingly amassed and edited by our old friend Alan Thomas.

"I'm surprised that it gave you any ideas at all," said Larry.

"Well, it did. I thought of doing a kind of compilation thing. I've got a lot of material that I haven't been able to use in a book. I thought of putting it all together and making a book out of it."

"Good idea," said Larry, pouring himself out another glass of retsina. "Never waste good material."

He held his glass up to the light and admired the color. Then he looked at me and his eyes twinkled mischievously.

"I tell you what," he said. "You could call it *Fillets of Plaice*."

And that is exactly what I have done.

FILLETS OF PLAICE

❉ The Birthday Party ❉

IT HAD BEEN a very long, hot summer even by Corfu standards. For several months no rain had fallen and from sunrise to sunset the sun glowered down upon the island out of a madonna-blue sky. Everything was parched and desiccated and the heat was intense. It had been rather an exhausting summer from our point of view. Larry, with characteristic generosity, had invited a large number of his artistic friends to stay. They came, in fact, in such droves that Mother was forced to employ two extra maids and she spent most of her time in our vast, gloomy, subterranean kitchen rushing from stove to stove to cook enough food to keep this army of playwrights, poets, authors, and artists well fed and happy. Now we had just seen the last of them off and the family were relaxing on the balcony, sipping iced tea and looking out over the still, blue sea.

"Well, thank goodness that's over," said Mother, sipping her tea and straightening her glasses. "Really, Larry dear, I do wish you wouldn't invite all these people. It's been terribly fatiguing."

"Well, it wouldn't have been if you'd organized it properly," said Larry. "After all, they all wanted to help."

Mother glared at him.

"Can you imagine that crowd down in my kitchen

3

helping?" she asked. "It was bad enough at mealtimes, let alone having them under my feet in the kitchen. No, I want to have a peaceful time for the rest of the summer. I don't feel I want to do anything. I feel absolutely depleted."

"Well, nobody's asking you to do anything," said Larry.

"Are you sure you haven't invited anybody else?" asked Mother.

"Not that I can think of," said Larry carelessly.

"Well, if they come, they can just jolly well stay in hotels," said Mother. "I've had enough."

"I don't know what you're getting so belligerent about," said Larry in a pained tone of voice. "I thought they were an awfully nice crowd."

"*You* didn't have to cook for them," said Mother. "I just don't want to see that kitchen again. I'd just like to go somewhere and get away from it all."

"That's a jolly good idea," said Larry.

"What?" Mother inquired.

"Getting away from it all."

"Getting away where?" asked Mother suspiciously.

"Well, how about a boat trip to the mainland?" Larry suggested.

"By Jove, that's an idea!" said Leslie.

"What a good idea!" said Margo. "Do let's do that, Mother. Ooh, I know! We could go over there to celebrate your birthday."

"Well," said Mother uncertainly, "I don't know about that. Whereabouts on the mainland?"

"Oh, we just hire a benzina," said Larry airily, "and sort of float down the coast, stopping where we want to. We can take enough food for two or three days and just loll about, have fun, relax."

"Well, it *sounds* very nice," said Mother. "I suppose Spiro could arrange a boat?"

"Oh, yes," said Leslie, "Spiro will do all that."

"Well," said Mother, "I must say it would make a change, wouldn't it?"

"There's nothing like sea air when you're feeling a bit jaded," said Larry. "Bucks you up no end. And we could perhaps take a few people along to sort of stimulate us, liven us up a bit."

"Now, not more people," said Mother.

"Well, I didn't mean more *people*," Larry explained. "I meant Theodore, for example."

"Theodore wouldn't come," said Margo. "You know he's prone to seasickness."

"Well, he might," said Larry. "And then there's Donald and Max."

Mother wavered. She was very fond of Donald and Max.

"Well, I . . . I suppose *they* could come," she said.

"And Sven should be back by then," said Larry. "He'd like to come, I'm sure."

"Oh, I don't mind Sven," said Mother. "I like Sven."

"And I could invite Mactavish," said Leslie.

"Oh God, not that awful man," Larry said disdainfully.

"I don't see why you call him an awful man," said Leslie belligerently. "We have to put up with your awful friends. Why shouldn't you put up with mine?"

"Now, now, dears," said Mother peaceably, "don't argue. I suppose we could ask Mactavish, if you really want to have him. But I don't really see what you see in him, Leslie."

"He's a jolly good pistol shot," said Leslie, as if this was sufficient explanation.

"And I could invite Leonora," said Margo excitedly.

"Now look! Stop it, all of you," said Mother. "By the time you're finished you'll have the boat sinking. I thought the whole idea was to go away and have a rest from people."

"But these aren't *people*," said Larry, "these are friends. All the difference in the world."

"Well, just let's leave it at that number then," said Mother. "If I have to cook enough food for three days, that's quite sufficient."

"I'll see Spiro, when he comes, about the boat," said Leslie.

"What about taking the ice-box?" asked Larry.

Mother put on her spectacles again and looked at him.

"Taking the ice-box?" she asked. "Are you joking?"

"No, of course I'm not joking," said Larry. "We want iced drinks and butter and things like that."

"But, Larry dear," said Mother, "don't be *ridiculous*. You know what a major operation it was to get it into the house at all. We can't move it."

"I don't see why not," said Larry. "It's perfectly possible if we put our minds to it."

"Which generally means," said Leslie, "that you give orders and let everybody else do the work."

"Nonsense," said Larry, "it's perfectly simple. After all, if it was got into the house, it must be possible to get it out again."

The ice-box they were referring to was Mother's pride and joy. In those days in Corfu none of the outlying villas could boast of electricity, and if such a thing as a kerosene refrigerator had been invented, it certainly hadn't reached Corfu. Mother, having decided that it was unhygienic to live without a refrigerator, had drawn a rather shaky plan of an ice-box similar to the ones that she had used in India when she was a girl. She had given the sketch to Spiro and asked him whether he could have something similar made.

Spiro had scowled over it and then said, "Leaves its to me, Mrs. Durrells," and waddled off into town.

Two weeks had passed and then one morning a large cart drawn by four horses, with six men sitting on the front, appeared up the drive. On the back of the cart was a monstrous ice-box. It was fully six feet long and four feet wide and four feet high. It was built out of inch-thick plank and had been lined with zinc, and then saw-dust had been padded down between the zinc and the wood. It took the six men, brawny though they were, the entire morning to get it into the larder. In the end we had to take the French windows off the drawing room and carry it in that way. Once installed, it dwarfed everything. Periodically Spiro would bring great, long, dripping blocks of ice from town in his car and we would stock the thing up with it. In this way we could keep butter and milk and eggs fresh for a considerable length of time.

"No," said Mother firmly, "I'm not having the ice-box moved. Apart from anything else, you might damage its mechanism."

"It hasn't *got* any mechanism," Larry pointed out.

"Well, it might get damaged," said Mother. "No, I've quite made up my mind. We're not having it moved. We can take enough ice with us. If we wrap it up in sacks and things, it should last."

Larry said nothing, but I saw the gleam in his eye.

As it was Mother's birthday that we were going to celebrate while on the ocean, we all were busy working out our presents for her. After some thought, I had decided to give her a butterfly net since she evinced such a great interest in my butterfly collection. Margo bought her a dress length of material which she rather wanted herself. Larry bought her a book which he wanted to read, and Leslie bought her a small pearl-handled revolver. As he explained to me, it would make her feel safe when we left her alone in the house. As his room was already a bristling armory of guns of various shapes and sizes, none of which Mother knew how to use, I felt this was rather a curious choice, but I said nothing.

The plans for our great venture went forward. Food was ordered and cooked. Sven, Donald and Max, Leonora, and Mactavish were alerted. Theodore at first, as we had expected, said that he wouldn't come as he was so prone to seasickness, but as we told him that there were a number of interesting ponds and little streams that we could stop at on the coastline, he wavered. Ardent freshwater biologist as he was, he felt it might be worth the risk in order to investigate these, so he decided to come after all.

We had arranged that the benzina would come to the villa and there we would load it up. Then it would go back into the town, we would follow in the car, pick up all the other members of our party, and set off from there.

The morning that the benzina was supposed to arrive Mother and Margo had gone into town to do some last-minute shopping with Spiro. I was upstairs, putting a dead snake into spirits, when I heard strange thumping and banging noises downstairs. Wondering what on earth was afoot, I sped down. The noise seemed to be coming from the larder. I went in there and found six stalwart young village lads being directed by Leslie and Larry, trying to move the monstrous ice-box. They had managed to shift it some considerable way, having knocked half the plaster off one wall, and Yani had dropped one end on his toe and was hobbling around with a bloodstained handkerchief tied around his foot.

"What on earth are you doing?" I asked. "You know Mother doesn't want that moved."

"Now, you shut up and don't interfere," said Leslie. "We've got everything under control."

"Just go *away*," said Larry. "Go *away* and don't get in the way. Why don't you go down to the jetty and see whether the benzina's come?"

I left them sweating and heaving on the giant ice-box and made my way down the hillside, across the road, and onto our jetty. Standing at the end of it, I peered hopefully out towards the town of Corfu and there, sure enough, heading along the coast, came a benzina. I watched it as it drew closer and closer and wondered why it didn't come in to shore towards the jetty. It was quite obvious that it was going to go straight past. Spiro, I thought, couldn't have given the right instructions. I jumped up and down on the end of the jetty and waved my arms and shouted, and eventually I attracted the attention of the man in the boat.

In a leisurely fashion he turned the benzina's nose in and brought it up to the jetty, flung his anchor over the back, and let the nose of the boat bump gently against the woodwork.

"Good morning," I said. "Are you Taki?"

He was a little, fat, brown man with pale, golden, chrysanthemum-colored eyes. He shook his head.

"No," he said, "I'm Taki's cousin."

9

"Oh," I said, "oh, well, that's all right. They won't be a minute. They're just bringing the ice-box down."

"The ice-box?" he asked.

"Yes, the ice-box. It's rather large," I said, "but I think it'll go *there*."

"All right," he said resignedly.

At that moment, at the top of the hillside, appeared the sweating, panting, arguing group of peasant lads, carrying in their midst the ice-box, with Larry and Leslie dancing around them. They looked like a group of drunken dung beetles with a monstrous ball of dung. Slowly, slipping and sliding and almost falling, and at one point almost dropping the ice-box so it rolled down the hill, they made their way down to the road, paused for a rest, and then got onto the jetty.

The jetty was constructed out of weather-beaten planks and the upright struts were of cypress wood. It was a strong enough jetty in its way, but it had been in existence for some considerable time. It had not, moreover, been designed to carry ice-boxes of the calibre of this one, and so as the panting, sweating crowd of peasants got to the middle of it there was a roaring crash and they and the ice-box fell into the sea.

"Bloody fools!" shouted Larry. "Bloody fools! Why didn't you look where you were going!"

"It's not their fault. The planks gave way," said Leslie.

Yani had fallen so that both his feet were under the ice-box, but fortunately the bottom of the sea was very sandy at this point, so instead of his legs being crushed they were just pressed into a soft base.

With considerable effort and much shouting and altercation they managed to get the ice-box onto the jetty again. And then, using the round cypress poles from the broken part of the jetty as rollers, they rolled it down and got it on board the benzina.

"There," said Larry, "quite simple. I told you it would be. Well now, you hang on here, Gerry, and we'll go back to the villa and fetch the rest of the things."

Laughing and triumphant, the peasant boys went up the hillside with Larry and Leslie to fetch the rest of our equipment. I watched them going so I wasn't taking much notice of the benzina. Suddenly I heard the rattle of the anchor and I turned round and found that the man had pulled the boat well out from the jetty and was just hauling his anchor on board.

"Hoy!" I cried. "What are you doing?"

"Pulling in my anchor," he said. He seemed to be a fairly literal sort of bloke.

"But where are you going?" I asked.

"Gouvia," he said, and started the engine.

"But you can't go to Gouvia," I shouted. "You can't. You're supposed to take us to the mainland. And you've got our ice-box!"

But the noise of the engine was too loud and, in any case, even if he heard me he ignored me. He turned the bow of the benzina seawards and chug-chug-chugged off along the coast. I watched him with dismay. What on earth could we do now?

I ran back along the jetty, jumped over the broken part, and scampered up onto the road. I had to get up to the villa as soon as possible and tell Larry what had happened. Just at that moment they appeared at the top of the hill, carrying picnic baskets and various other things. And almost at the same moment Spiro's car drove up along the road with Mother and Margo in the back.

Larry and Leslie and their peasant helpers arrived at the road simultaneously with the car.

"What are you doing, dear?" asked Mother, getting out of the car.

"We're just bringing the things down to put them in the benzina," said Larry. And then he glanced at the jetty.

"Where the hell is it?" he asked.

"That's what I was trying to tell you," I said. "He's gone."

"What do you mean, he's *gone?*" asked Leslie. "How could he have gone?"

"Well, he has," I said. "Look, there he is."

They peered and saw the benzina disappearing down the coast.

"But where's he gone *to?*" asked Larry.

"He said he was going to Gouvia."

"Well, what's he going to Gouvia *for?* He's supposed to take us to the mainland."

"That's what I told him but he wouldn't take any notice of me."

"But he's got the ice-box," said Leslie.

"He's got the *what?*" asked Mother.

"The ice-box," said Larry irritably. "We put the bloody ice-box on board and he's got that."

"I told you not to *touch* that ice-box," said Mother. "I told you not to move it. Really, Larry, you do make me angry."

"Oh, Mother, do stop fussing," said Larry. "The thing is to get the damn thing back again now. What do you think this fool is up to, Spiro? You employed him."

"No, it wasn't Taki," I said. "It was his cousin."

"That's not Taki's benzinas," said Spiro, scowling thoughtfully.

"Well, what are we going to *do?*" asked Mother, distraught.

"We'll have to go after him," said Larry.

"I'll takes your mothers up to the house," said Spiro, "and then I'll goes to Gouvia."

"But you can't bring the ice-box back in a car," said Larry.

Just at that moment the sound of another benzina engine made itself heard and, looking round, we saw a second boat approaching from the town.

"Ah," said Spiro, "that's Taki's benzinas."

"Well, let him give chase," said Larry. "Let him give chase. As soon as he gets here, tell him to give chase and get that bloody icebox back. I don't know what that fool was playing at, taking it away like that."

"Didn't he show any surprise," asked Leslie of me, "when you asked him to put the ice-box on board?"

"No," I said, "he just looked blank."

"As well he might," said Mother. "I would look blank, too, in similar circumstances."

When Taki's boat eventually made the jetty we explained the predicament to him. He was a nice, wiry little man and grinned amicably, showing large quantities of gold teeth.

"Here, these boys had better go with him," said Larry. "Otherwise we'll never get the ice-box from one benzina to the other."

The six peasant boys, delighted at the idea of a sea trip, clambered on board chattering and laughing excitedly.

"Leslie, you'd better go with them," said Larry.

"All right," said Leslie. "I suppose I'd better."

He got on board the boat and it chugged off in pursuit of the first one.

"I simply can't understand it," said Mother. "What did the man think he was doing?"

"Oh, Mother," said Margo, "you know what it's like in Corfu. Everybody's mad,"

"Yes, but not *that* mad," said Mother. "You don't bring a benzina in and pick up a complete stranger's ice-box and go off with it, just like that."

"Maybes hes comes from Zante," said Spiro, as if this explained everything.

"Well, I don't know. Really!" said Mother. "What a start to the whole thing! You children do make me angry."

"Now, I think that's unfair, Mother," said Margo. "After all, Larry and Leslie weren't to know they'd put it on the wrong benzina."

"They should have asked," said Mother. "We might never get it back."

"Don'ts yous worrys, Mrs. Durrells," said Spiro, scowling. "I'll gets its backs. Yous comes ups to the house."

So we all went up to the house and waited there. After about three and a half hours Mother's nerves were in shreds.

"I'm sure they've dropped it into the sea," she said. "Really, I shall never forgive you, Larry. I explicitly told you not to move the ice-box."

At that moment we heard dimly, far away, the put-put-put of a benzina. I ran out with the field glasses and peered out across the sea. Sure enough, there was Taki's benzina coming towards the jetty, with the ice-box carefully installed on it. I ran back with the news to Mother.

"Well," she said, "that's something, I suppose. Now perhaps we can get off. Really, I feel as though I've aged another year even though I haven't had my birthday."

So we carried all our things once more down to the jetty and packed them on board the benzina. Then we piled into the car and drove into town.

In town we found our friends gathered together having a drink under the cool shade of the columns on the Esplanade. There was Sven, who looked like a great, moon-faced baby with his almost bald head and his tattered wispy fringe of grey hair, clasping his precious accordion to him – an instrument which he never travelled without. There was Theodore, immaculately clad in a suit, with a Panama hat, his beard and moustache twinkling golden in the sun. Beside his chair he had his cane with a little net on the end of it and his box containing his precious test tubes and bottles for collecting. There was Donald, who looked pale and aristocratic; Max, tall and gangling, with curly hair and a brown moustache perched like a butterfly on his upper lip; Leonora, blonde, nubile, and very beautiful; and Mactavish, a stocky man with a brown, lined face and thinning grey hair.

We apologized for being late, which nobody seemed to have noticed, had a drink while Spiro collected some of the more perishable goods, and made our way down to where the benzina awaited us.

We climbed on board, the final parcels of foodstuff were packed away in the ice-box, the engine was started, and we cruised out across the placid water.

"I've bought some, um . . . you know . . . seasick pills," said Theodore gravely, casting a suspicious glance at the water, which looked as though it had been painted. "I though perhaps there might be a little motion, you know, and as I'm such a bad sailor I thought I'd take a precaution."

"Well, if there's any motion, you can give me one," said Mother. "I'm a very bad sailor, too."

"Muzzer von't get seasick," said Max, patting her on the shoulder. "I von't let Muzzer get seasick."

"I don't see how you're going to stop it," said Mother.

"Garlic," said Max, "garlic. It's an old Austrian remedy. It is excellent,"

"What do you mean – raw garlic?" said Margo. "How disgusting."

"No, no, Margo dear, it is not disgusting," said Max. "It is very good for you, very good indeed."

"I can't stand men who smell of garlic," said Margo. "They simply blow you to pieces."

"But if you took de garlic too," said Max, "den you could blow dem to pieces."

"Damned bad form, eating garlic," said Donald. "Damned bad form. Only Continentals do it."

"It's supposed to be, um . . . exceedingly good for one," said Theodore, "according to medical evidence."

"Well, I always put it in the food when I'm cooking," said Mother. "I think it adds to the flavor."

"But it's such a terribly dreary smell," said Leonora, draping herself like a Persian cat on the deck. "I travelled on a bus out to Perema the other day and, my dear, I nearly suffocated. Everybody was chewing the most enormous cloves of garlic and breathing it all back at me. I felt quite faint by the time we got there."

Sven unhitched his accordion and hung it round his waist.

"My dear Mrs. Durrell, what would you like me to play?" he inquired.

"Oh, er . . . I don't mind, Sven," said Mother. "Something gay."

"How about 'There Is a Tavern in the Town'?" suggested Theodore. This was the one tune that he could hear incessantly with great pleasure.

"Very well," said Sven, and started playing.

Leslie and Mactavish were up in the bows. Periodically Mactavish would do a few knee-bends or press-ups. He was a health fiend, among other things. He had been in the Royal Canadian Mounted Police at one time during his career and seldom let you forget it. He always endeavored to be the life and soul of the party, and the thing that he was proudest of was the fact that he was in tip-top physical condition. He would slap his stomach and say, "Look at that, look at that! Not bad for a man of forty-five, eh?"

So the benzina chugged its way across the channel that separated Corfu from the mainland, with Theodore vigorously singing "There Is a Tavern in the Town."

The trip over seemed extraordinarily short for me. There was so much to watch for – flying fish, sea gulls – and I was constantly having to drag Theodore away from the adult company to ask his erudite advice on bits of seaweed and similar things of interest that were passing the boat.

Then eventually we reached the extraordinary brown and eroded coast between Albania and Corfu, which spread on into Greece, and as we drew closer and closer to the coast we passed towering pinnacles of rock like the carunculated, melted remains of a million multicolored candles. Eventually, as night was falling, we discovered a bay that looked as though it had been bitten out of the hard rock by some gigantic sea monster. It was a perfect half-moon, and here we thought we would make landfall. The sand was white, the cliffs tall and protective, and so the benzina was brought gently in, the anchor was thrown over the side, and we came to a halt.

This was the moment when the ice-box came into its own. Out of it Mother and Spiro unpacked an incredible assortment of foodstuffs: legs of lamb stuffed with garlic, lobsters, and various extraordinary things Mother had made which she called curry puffs. Some of them were in fact curry puffs, but others were stuffed with different delicacies. And so we lay around on the deck and gorged ourselves.

In the foreparts of the boat we had a great pile of watermelons that looked like an array of pudgy footballs, green with whitish stripes on them. Periodically one of these would be popped into the ice-box and then brought out so that we could cut it open, and the pink and beautiful inside was as crisp as a water ice cream. I got a certain amount of pleasure out of spitting the black pips from the watermelons over the side of the boat and watching all the small fish rush madly towards them, and then they would mouth them and reject them. There were some bigger ones, however, who, to my astonishment, came up and absorbed them like Hoovers.

After that we all bathed, with the exception of Mother, Theodore, and Sven, who had an esoteric conversation on the subject of witchcraft, haunted houses, and vampires, while Spiro and Taki did the washing up.

It was fantastic to dive from the side of the boat into the dark waters, for as you hit them they burst into a firework display of greeny-gold phosphorescence, so that you felt you were diving into a fire. Swimming underwater, people left trails of phosphorescence behind them like a million tiny stars, and when Leonora, who was the last one to come aboard, hauled herself up, her whole body for a brief moment looked as though it was encased in gold.

"My God, she's lovely," said Larry admiringly, "but I'm sure she's a lesbian. She resists all my advances."

"Larry dear," said Mother, "you shouldn't say things like that about people."

"She's certainly very lovely," said Sven, "so beautiful, in fact, that it almost makes me wish I weren't a homosexual. However, there are advantages to being homosexual."

"I think to be bisexual is best," said Larry; "then you've got the best of both worlds, as it were."

"Larry dear," said Mother. "you may find this conversation fascinating, but I don't and I do wish you wouldn't talk about it in front of Gerry."

Mactavish was doing a series of complicated keep-fit exercises in the front of the boat.

"God, that man does irritate me," said Larry, pouring out some more wine. "What's he keep fit *for*? He never appears to do anything."

"Really, dear," said Mother, "do stop making comments about people. It's very embarrassing on a small boat like this. He might hear you."

"Well, I wouldn't mind if he kept fit in order to go around raping all the girls in Corfu," said Larry, "but he never *does* anything."

While doing his exercises, Mactavish was, for about the eighty-fourth time, telling Leslie, who was lounging near him, of his experiences as a Mountie. All of them were very thrilling and inevitably ended with Mactavish getting his man.

"Ooooooh!" screeched Margo suddenly, with such vehemence that we all jumped and Larry upset his glass of wine.

"I wish you wouldn't make those sudden gull-like cries," he said irritably.

"But I just remembered," said Margo, "it's Mother's birthday tomorrow."

"Muzzer has a birzday tomorrow?" said Max. "But vy didn't you tell us?"

"Well, that's why we came over here – to celebrate Mother's birthday, to give her a holiday," said Margo.

"But if Muzzer has a birzday, ve have no present to give her," said Max.

"Oh, don't worry about that," said Mother; "I really shouldn't be having birthdays at my age."

"Damned bad form to come to a birthday party without bringing a present," said Donald. "Damned bad form."

"Oh, now, do stop fussing," said Mother; "you make me quite embarrassed."

"I shall play to you endlessly throughout the day, my dear Mrs. Durrell," said Sven. "I shall give you a birthday gift of music."

Although Sven could play such things as "There Is a Tavern in the Town," his real favorite was Bach, and I could see Mother wince visibly at the thought of a whole day spent with Sven playing Bach to her.

"No, no," she said hurriedly, "you mustn't make a fuss."

"Vell, ve vill have a tremendous celebration tomorrow," said Max. "Ve vill find a special place and ve vill celebrate Muzzer's birzday in true Continental style."

Presently the mattresses that we had brought with us were unrolled, and gradually we all drifted into sleep as a moon as red as a robin's breast edged its way up over the mountains above us and gradually turned to lemon yellow and then silver.

The following morning at dawn we were all startled – and, in consequence, irritated – by Sven waking us playing "Happy Birthday to You" on his accordion. He was crouched on his knees, gazing raptly into Mother's face to see the effect it would have. Mother, not being used to having an accordion played six inches away from her ear, woke with a squeak of alarm.

"What's the matter? What's the matter? Are we sinking?" she gasped.

"Sven, for God's sake," said Larry, "it's five o'clock."

"Ah," said Max drowsily, "but it's Muzzer's birzday. Ve must now start to celebrate. Now, come, ve all sing togezzer." He leapt to his feet, banged his head on the mast, and then waved his long arms and said, "Now, Sven, play it again. All togezzer now."

Sleepily, reluctantly, we all had to sing "Happy Birthday to You," while Mother sat there making desperate attempts not to fall asleep again.

"Shalls I makes some teas, Mrs. Durrells?" asked Spiro.

"I think that would be a very good idea," said Mother.

Our various presents were brought out and given to her, and she expressed delight at each one, including the pearl-handled revolver, though she did say that she felt Leslie ought to keep it in his room as it would be safer there. If, as he had suggested, she kept it under her pillow, it might suddenly go off in the night and do her a serious injury.

The application of tea and a quick swim revived us all. The sun was now coming up and the night mist was being drawn up from the water in pale skeins. After a breakfast consisting mainly of fruit and hard-boiled eggs, the engine was started and we chugged off down the coast.

"Ve must find de most superb spot for Muzzer's lunch," said Max. "It must be a Garden of Eden."

"By Jove, yes," said Donald, "we must find a really superb spot."

"Then I can play to you, my dear Mrs. Durrell," said Sven.

Presently we chugged our way round a headland that looked as though it had been constructed out of immense bricks of red, gold, and white rock, with a huge umbrella pine perched on top of it, clinging precariously to the edge and leaning dangerously seaward. As we rounded it, we saw that it guarded a small bay where there was a tiny village, and on the slopes of the mountain behind the village were the remains of an old Venetian fort.

"That looks interesting," said Larry. "Let's pop in here and have a look at it."

"I wouldn't goes theres, Master Larrys," said Spiro, scowling.

"Why ever not?" asked Larry. "It looks like a charming little village and that fort looks interesting."

"They's practically Turks," said Spiro.

"What d'you mean, 'practically'?" said Larry. "Either you're a Turk or you're not a Turk."

"Wells, theys acts like Turks," said Spiro. "not likes Greeks, so reallys they's Turks."

Everybody was a bit confused by this piece of logic.

"But even if they *are* Turks," said Larry, "what does it matter?"

"Some of these, um . . . um . . . remoter villages have a very strong Turkish influence since the Turkish invasion of Greece," said Theodore knowledgeably. "They have adopted many of the Turkish customs, and so in some of these out-of-the-way places, as Spiro quite rightly points out, they are really more Turkish than Greek."

"But what the hell does it matter?" asked Larry in exasperation.

"They sometimes don't particularly care for foreigners," said Theodore.

"Well, they can't object to our stopping and looking at the fort," said Larry, "and in any case, the village is so small I should think we outnumber them by about three to one. Besides, if they look belligerent we can always send Mother ahead with her pearl-handled revolver. That's bound to quell them."

"Yous really wants to goes?" asked Spiro.

"Yes," said Larry. "Are you afraid of a few Turks?"

Spiro's face became suffused with blood to a point where I thought he was liable to have a stroke.

"You shouldn'ts says things like thats, Master Larrys," he said. "I'm not afraids of any son-of-a-bitch Turks."

He turned and stomped off to the end of the boat and gave Taki instructions to head for the little jetty.

"Larry dear, you shouldn't say things like that," said Mother. "You've hurt his feelings. You know how strongly they feel about the Turks."

"But they're not bloody Turks," said Larry, "they're Greeks."

"Technically speaking, I suppose you could call them Greeks," said Theodore, "but in these remoter places they have become so like Turks as to be almost indistinguishable. It's a curious amalgam, as it were."

As we nosed our way in to the jetty, a small boy who had been sitting there fishing picked up his rod and line and ran off into the village.

"You don't think that he's gone to alert them, do you?" asked Leonora nervously. "I mean, so that they can come out with guns and things?"

"Oh, don't be so damned silly," said Larry.

"Let me go first," said Mactavish. "I'm used to this sort of situation. Frequently met it among the outlying

23

Indian tribes in Canada while I was tracking a man down. I have a knack for getting on with primitive people."

Larry groaned and was about to make a sarcastic remark but was quelled by a vicious look from Mother.

"Now," said Mactavish, taking charge of operations, "the best thing to do is to get onto the jetty and stroll about a bit admiring things as though, er . . . as though . . . er. . ."

"As though we were tourists?" Larry suggested innocently.

"I was about to *say*," said Mactavish, "as though we had no evil intentions."

"Dear God," said Larry, "one would think this were Darkest Africa."

"Larry dear, do be quiet," said Mother. "I'm sure Mr. Mactavish knows best. After all, it *is* my birthday."

So we all trooped out onto the jetty and stood for some moments pointing in different directions and carrying on ridiculous conversations with each other.

"Now," said Mactavish, "forward into the village."

Leaving Spiro and Taki in charge of the boat, we trooped off.

The village consisted of some thirty or forty houses, all tiny, whitewashed and gleaming, some of them with trellises of green vine, some shrouded in cloaks of purple bougainvillea.

With a brisk, military walk Mactavish led the way, looking like an intrepid member of the French Foreign Legion about to take over an unruly Arab settlement, and we all ambled after him.

In the village there was only one main street, if it could be dignified with that term, and off it ran several tiny alleyways between the houses. As we approached one of these passages, a woman wearing a yashmak rushed out of a house, gave us a horrified glance, and disappeared down the alleyway at a hurried pace. I had never seen a yashmak before so I was vastly intrigued.

"What was she wearing on her face?" I inquired. "Is she bandaged up for some reason?"

"No, no," said Theodore, "she's wearing a yashmak. If they are very Turkish in this village you will find that most of the women wear them to cover their faces."

"I always thought it was a bloody silly idea," said Larry. "If a woman's got a pretty face, she should show it. The only thing I would advocate is a gag if she talked too much."

The street led inevitably to what was the hub of any village – a tiny square dominated by an enormous and very beautiful umbrella pine, and in its shade a series of tables and chairs. Here was the tiny café which, like the local pub in an English village, dispensed not only foodstuffs but wine and gossip and slander in equal quantities. It was very curious to me that as our cavalcade had passed through the village we had seen not a living soul except the woman. If it had been one of the remoter villages of Corfu, we would have been surrounded by now by a vociferous and fascinated crowd of inhabitants. However, when we came to the village square we saw – or at least we thought we saw – the reason, for most of the little tables under the pine tree were occupied by men, most of whom were elderly, with impressive long white beards, wearing baggy pants, tattered shirts, and charukias, the curious shoes of bright red leather with upturned toes decorated with highly colored pompons. They greeted the arrival of our group in the square with complete silence. They just sat and looked at us.

"Aha!" said Mactavish in a loud and cheerful voice. *"Kalimera, kalimera, kalimera!"*

If it had been a Greek village there would have been an immediate response to his cry of "good morning." Some would have responded with *"Kalimera"*; some would have said, "We are glad you have come"; and others would have said, *"Herete,"* which means "be happy." Instead, there was no reaction except that one or two of the older men bowed their heads gravely in our direction.

"Well, now," said Mactavish, "let's get a few tables together, have a few drinks, and once they get used to us I'm sure they'll rally round."

"I don't think I really like it," said Mother nervously. "Don't you think that Margo, Leonora, and I ought to go back to the boat? I mean, it's all men and no women."

"Oh, nonsense, Mother. Stop fussing," said Larry.

"I think," said Theodore, glancing up lovingly at the huge umbrella pine above us, "I think that's why that small boy ran into the village. In some of these remoter villages, you know, the women have to stay in the houses. And so he went, you know, to warn them. Also the sight of, um . . . um . . . er . . . the er . . . ladies of the party must be, er . . . you know, um . . . unusual to them."

As Mother, Margo, and Leonora were not wearing yashmaks and Margo and Leonora were wearing rather dashing cotton dresses which left a considerable portion of their anatomy visible, this was not altogether surprising.

We joined several tables together, placed chairs around them, and sat down. The groups of men, who, contrary to Larry's expectations, outnumbered us by about five to one, continued to sit there silently, gazing at us as impassively as lizards. After we had waited for

some considerable time, making rather haphazard conversation, an elderly man shuffled out of the café and
came with obvious reluctance to our table. By now
thoroughly unnerved, we all said *kalimera* in unison
with various degrees of nervous enthusiasm. To our
infinite relief, he said *kalimera* back.

"Now," said Mactavish, who rather prided himself
on his command of the Greek language, "we'll have a
little drink and some *meze*."

It should have been unnecessary for him to add the
request for *meze*, for this includes such things as olives,
nuts, hard-boiled eggs, cucumbers, cheese, and similar
little plates which, if you ordered a drink in Greece,
were automatically served. But it seemed in the circumstances that even an ex-Mountie was beginning to
become slightly rattled.

"Yes," said the café owner gravely. "What drink
would you require?"

Mactavish took orders for our drinks, which ranged
from ginger beer through ouzo to brandy and retsina.
He translated all this to the café owner.

"I have only red wine," said the café owner.

An exasperated look spread across Mactavish's face.

"Well then, bring us red wine and *meze*," he said.

The café owner gave a little nod of his head and
shuffled back to the interior of his gloomy little shop.

"Now why," asked Mactavish, "should he ask me
what we wanted to drink when he knew perfectly well
he'd only got red wine?"

Mactavish loved the Greeks dearly and had taken the
trouble to speak their language quite fluently, but he
could never quite come to terms with their logic.

"It's perfectly obvious," said Larry exasperatedly.
"He wanted to find out what you wanted to drink and

if you had wanted red wine he would have gone and got it for you."

"Yes, but why not just say he's got red wine in the first place and nothing else?"

"But that doesn't happen in Greece," Larry explained patiently. "It's too logical."

We sat at our table with all those inimical eyes fastened on us, feeling rather like a group of actors on a stage who had all simultaneously forgotten their lines. Presently the old man shuffled out carrying a battered tin tray which bore upon it, for some obscure reason, a portrait of Queen Victoria, and he placed on the table some little plates of small black olives and chunks of white goat cheese, two flagons of wine, and a series of glasses that, although clean, were so chipped and worn with use that they looked as though they could give you any one of a number of interesting diseases.

"They do not seem very happy in dis village," observed Max.

"What do you expect?" said Donald. "Lot of damned foreigners. Now, if this were England it would be different."

"Yes," said Larry sarcastically, "we'd be doing Morris dancing with them in next to no time."

Although the concentrated stare of our male audience had not really changed, it had now in our nervous state begun to look positively malevolent.

"Music," said Sven, "it soothes the savage beast. I will play you a tune."

"Well, for God's sake, play something cheerful," said Larry. "If you start playing Bach to them I can see them all going and getting their muzzle-loaders."

Sven hitched his accordion into position and played

a very charming little polka which should have softened any Greek's heart. But our audience remained unmoved, though it seemed there was a slight lessening of tension in the air.

"I really do think that Margo, Leonora, and I ought to go back to the boat," said Mother.

"No, no, my dear Mrs. Durrell," said Mactavish. "I assure you I know this situation so well. It takes times for these primitive people to adapt themselves to you. And now, since Sven's music has had no effect, I think the time has come for magic."

"Magic?" said Theodore, leaning forward and gazing at Mactavish intensely, deeply interested. "How do you mean, magic?"

"Conjuring," said Mactavish. "In my spare time I'm a bit of a conjurer."

"Dear God," groaned Larry, "why not give them strings of beads?"

"Oh, do shut up, Larry," hissed Margo. "Mactavish knows what he's doing."

"Well, I'm glad *you* think so," said Larry.

Mactavish strode off purposefully into the café and reappeared with a plate on which were four eggs. He placed these carefully on the table and stood back so the silent audience of villagers could observe.

"Now," he said, gesticulating in a professional conjurer's manner, "my first trick is the egg trick. May I borrow some sort of receptacle from one of you?"

"A handkerchief?" inquired Donald.

"No," said Mactavish, giving a glance at his audience of villagers, "I think something a little more spectacular. Mrs. Durrell, would you be kind enough to lend me your hat?"

During the summer months Mother used to wear a large straw hat that, in view of her minuteness, made her look somewhat like an animated mushroom.

"I don't want egg all over it," she said.

"No, no, I assure you," said Mactavish, "there's no danger."

Reluctantly, Mother removed her straw hat and handed it to Mactavish. With a great flourish he placed it on the table in front of him, glanced up to make sure the villagers were watching, took an egg and placed it carefully in the hat. Then he squeezed the brim together and gave the hat a resounding blow on the side of the table.

"If we save all the bits," said Larry, "I suppose we could have an omelet."

Mactavish, however, unfurled the hat and displayed it to us in such a way that the villagers could see that it was completely empty and egg-less. He then took a second egg and did precisely the same thing and again the hat was empty and egg-less. As he did the same again with the third egg, I saw animation starting to creep into the eyes of our village audience, and after the fourth egg one or two of the men were actually exchanging whispered remarks. With great flamboyance, Mactavish showed us all the completely empty and egg-less hat and showed it also to the villagers. He then placed it on the table and folded up the brim once more, then opened it and with perfect timing took out four absolutely intact eggs and placed them on the plate.

Even Larry was impressed. Of course, it was a simple job of what conjurers call palming. That is to say, you appear to put an object into something, while in actual fact you keep it in your hand and then conceal it on some part of your anatomy. I had seen it done with watches and other objects but I had never seen it done quite so skilfully with four eggs, which are, after all, not the easiest things to conceal and are the easiest things to break during such a trick, thus spoiling the whole effect.

Mactavish bowed to our solemn clapping and, to our great astonishment, there were even a few desultory claps from the villagers. Some of the older men, in fact, who had slightly defective eyesight switched tables with the younger ones so that they were closer to us.

"You see what I mean?" said Mactavish proudly. "Little bit of magic works wonders."

He then produced from his pocket a pack of cards and proceeded to go through the normal routine that conjurers use with cards, flourishing them up in the air so that they landed on his hand and spread out along his arm without a single card falling. The villagers were now really excited and from sitting on the opposite side of the square from us, they had now converged on us. The old men with defective eyesight had in fact become so intrigued that they had moved their chairs forward until they were almost sitting at our table.

It was obvious that Mactavish was enjoying himself immensely. He put an egg into his mouth, scrunched it up, and then opened his mouth wide to show that there was no egg there and produced it from his shirt pocket. Now there came a hearty round of applause from the villagers.

"Isn't he clever!" said Margo.

"I told you he was all right," said Leslie, "and he's a damned good pistol shot, too."

"I must ask him how he does these, um . . . illusions," said Theodore.

"I wonder if he knows how to saw a woman in half,"

31

said Larry thoughtfully, "I mean, so that you could get the half that functions but doesn't talk."

"Larry dear," said Mother, "not in front of Gerry."

Now came Mactavish's big moment. The front row of the village audience consisted entirely of old men with long white beards, and the younger men were standing in the background, craning their necks to watch his tricks. Mactavish strode forward to the oldest of the old men, who must surely have been the mayor of the village since we had noticed he had been given a special place of honor so that he could see the tricks more clearly. Mactavish stood there for a moment with his hands up, fingers spread wide, and said in Greek, "I will now show you another trick."

Swiftly, he reached down and produced from the old man's beard a drachma and threw the silver-colored coin on the ground. There was a gasp of astonishment from the assembled company. Then, having raised his arms and spread his fingers wide once more, he reached into the other side of the old man's beard and produced a five drachma piece, which he again, with a flourish, threw on the ground.

"Now," said Mactavish in Greek, holding up his hands once more, "you've seen how I have produced by magic this money from the mayor's beard. . . ."

"Can you produce more?" inquired the mayor in a quavering voice.

"Yes, yes," came a chorus of villagers, "can you produce more?"

"I will see what my magic can do," said Mactavish, by now completely carried away.

In rapid succession he produced from the mayor's beard a whole series of ten-drachma coins, which he threw on the mounting pile on the ground. In those days Greece was so poverty stricken that the shower of silver Mactavish was producing out of the mayor's beard represented a small fortune.

It was at that point that Mactavish overreached himself. He produced from the mayor's beard a fifty-drachma note. The *ah*'s of excitement were almost deafening. Encouraged by this, Mactavish produced four more fifty-drachma notes. The mayor sat there entranced. Periodically he would whisper a blessing to one or another of the many saints who he felt were producing this miracle.

"I think, you know," said Theodore in a tentative tone of voice, "it would be perhaps advisable not to produce any more."

But Mactavish was too flushed with enthusiasm to realize the danger. He produced a one-hundred-drachma note from the mayor's beard and the applause was deafening.

"Now," he said, "for my final trick," and he held up his hands once more to show that they were empty. He bent down and plucked out from the mayor's big beard a five-hundred-drachma note.

The amount of money that was now lying at the mayor's feet represented something like twenty or thirty pounds, which, to the average peasant anywhere in Greece, was a fortune beyond the dreams of avarice.

"There," said Mactavish, turning and smiling at us proudly, "it never fails."

"You certainly have got them in a very good mood," said Mother, who was by now completely relaxed.

"I told you not to worry, Mrs. Durrell," said Mactavish. Then he made his fatal mistake. He bent down, picked up all the money lying on the ground, and put it in his pocket.

Immediate uproar broke out.

"I, um . . . I had a sort of feeling this might happen," said Theodore.

The mayor had risen shakily to his feet and was brandishing his fist in Mactavish's face. Everybody else was shouting as indignantly as a disturbed rookery.

"But what's the matter?" asked Mactavish.

"You're stealing my money," said the mayor.

"I think," said Larry to Mother, "that now is the time for you, Leonora, and Margo to get back to the boat."

They left the table with alacrity and disappeared down the main street at a dignified trot.

"But what do you mean, *your* money?" Mactavish was saying earnestly to the mayor. "It was *my* money."

"How could it be your money if you found it in my beard?" asked the mayor.

Once again, Mactavish was defeated by the illogicality of the Greeks.

"But don't you see," he said painfully, "it was only magic? It was really my money."

"*No!*" came a chorus from the entire village. "If you found the money in *his* beard it's *his* money."

"But can't you see," said Mactavish desperately, "that I was doing tricks? It's all tricks."

"Yes, and the trick is to steal my money!" said the mayor.

"*Yes!*" came a rumbled agreement from the assembled population.

"Do you know," said Mactavish, turning desperately to Larry, "I think this old boy's senile. He can't see the point."

"You really are a bloody fool, you know," said Larry.

"Obviously, he thinks that if you got the money out of his beard it's his money."

"But it's not," said Mactavish obtusely. "It's *my* money. I palmed it."

"We know that, you fool, but *they* don't."

We were now surrounded by a throng of wild-looking and extremely indignant members of the community who were determined to see that justice was done to their mayor.

"Give him back his money," they all shouted, "or we'll stop your benzina from leaving!"

"We'll send to Athens for the police!" shouted one man.

As it would have taken several weeks to communicate with Athens and several weeks for a policeman to come back and investigate the thing – if, indeed, one was ever sent – the whole situation was taking on alarming proportions.

"I think, um. . ." said Theodore, "the best thing would be for you to give him the money."

"That's what I have always said about foreigners," said Donald. "Excitable. Rapacious, too. Just like Max here who is always borrowing money from me and never paying it back."

"Now do not let us start to quarrel too," said Max. "Dere is enough quarrel here for everybody."

"Really," said Larry, "Theodore's is the best suggestion. You must give it back to him, Mactavish."

"But it's twenty pounds!" said Mactavish. "And after all, it was only a trick."

"Well, if you don't give it back to him," said Larry, "I think you've a very slim chance of getting out of here without being beaten up."

Mactavish drew himself up to his full height.

"I'm not afraid of a fight," he said.

"Oh, don't be stupid," said Larry in a weary tone of voice. "If all these stalwart young males go for you at once, you'll be torn to pieces."

"Well, we'll compromise," said Mactavish.

He took all the drachma pieces out of his pocket and handed them to the mayor.

"There," he said in Greek, "it was a trick and the money was not yours, but nevertheless, in order that you shall buy yourself some wine, I am giving you half of what I got from your beard."

"*No!*" roared the villagers in unison. "You'll give him everything!"

Mother, having got Leonora and Margo safely onto the boat, had come back to rescue me and was horrified at the sight of us surrounded by this threatening mob.

"Larry, Larry!" she shouted. "Save Gerry!"

"Oh, don't be stupid," Larry shouted back. "He's the only one of us who's not going to get beaten up."

This was perfectly true because in such a situation only accidentally would any Greek hurt a child.

"I suppose we could all get into a corner and face it out," said Donald. "It seems a bit much backing down to a lot of foreigners. I used to be quite good at boxing when I was at Eton."

"Um . . . have you, um . . . er . . . noticed that most of them are wearing knives?" inquired Theodore, as though he were discussing some museum specimen.

"Ah, I know how to fight wiz a knife," said Max.

"But you haven't got one," said Donald.

"True," said Max thoughtfully, "but if you knock one of dem down, I could get his knife off him and den we could fight dem."

"I don't think that would be a very wise thing to do," said Theodore.

During this, the uproar was still going on and Mactavish was still trying to persuade the mayor that they should split the proceeds of his beard fifty-fifty.

"Are you saving Gerry?" shouted Mother from the back of the crowd.

"Oh, shut up, Mother," yelled Larry. "You're only making things worse. Gerry's perfectly all right."

"I think, you know, judging from their tone of voice and the things that some of them are saying," said Theodore, "that we really will have to persuade Mactavish to give the money to the mayor. Otherwise we'll find ourselves in a rather unpleasant predicament."

"Are you saving Gerry?" shouted Mother again from behind the crowd.

"Oh, for Christ's sake!" said Larry.

He strode forward, seized Mactavish, delved into his pocket, produced the notes, and handed them to the mayor.

"Here! But I say! That's my money!" said Mactavish.

"Yes, and it's my life that you're mucking about with," said Larry.

He turned to the mayor.

"Now," he said in Greek, "that is the money that this kyrios by his magic found in your beard."

He turned to Mactavish, seized him by the shoulders, looked him straight in the eye and said, "You are to nod your head hard to whatever I say to you, do you understand?"

"Yes, yes," said Mactavish, startled by this sudden display of belligerence on the part of Larry.

"Well," said Larry. He paused and placed his hand

37

carefully over the part of Mactavish's anatomy that presumably concealed his heart.

> " 'Twas brillig, and the slithy toves
> Did gyre and gimble in the wabe:
> All mimsy were the borogoves,
> And the mome raths outgrabe."

Mactavish, startled not only by Larry's sudden masterly command of the situation but also by the fact that he didn't understand since he had never heard the poem before, nodded his head vehemently at the end of every line. Larry turned to the mayor.

"The *kyrios*," he said, placing his hand once more upon Mactavish's heart, "because he has a great heart, has agreed that you should have all the money, but on one condition. You all know how there are certain people who can find water in the ground."

There was an "ah" of affirmation from the crowd.

"These people are paid for their work," said Larry.

There was much nodding and "yes, yes, yes."

"But when they find the water," Larry continued, "the water must belong to everyone."

Now he was speaking a language they understood, for water and bread were the two life-giving things of any community.

"Sometimes the people who search for water find it and sometimes they don't," said Larry. "This *kyrios* sometimes finds money in people's beards and sometimes does not. He was lucky that you have a good mayor here and that he found money. He found nearly nine hundred drachmas. Now, because he is a good man and a kind man, he has agreed not to charge his normal fee."

There was an "ah" of pleasure, mixed with incomprehension at such generosity, from the crowd.

The Birthday Party

"But there is one thing he would ask you as a favor," said Larry – "that the mayor spend this money for the good of the whole village."

This was the point where the mayor looked extremely glum and the crowd applauded.

"Because," said Larry oratorically, having consumed vast quantities of wine, and getting into stride, "when you find money, as when you find water, it should belong to everyone."

The applause was so great that the few words the mayor mumbled were completely lost in it.

"I think, you know, perhaps now is the time to go," said Theodore, "on a high note, as it were."

We marched down the village street with the entire crowd following us, all of them jostling to pat Mactavish on the back or shake his hand. And so by the time we reached the jetty Mactavish was beginning to feel that he was the Mountie to end all Mounties and it had been well worth the loss of twenty pounds to have this adulation. In fact, our take-off was delayed for some minutes because the mayor insisted on kissing him on both cheeks and embracing him, whereupon all the other elders of the village had to do the same.

At last he joined us on board, flushed with success.

"I told you, didn't I?" he said. "It's just a matter of knowing how to deal with primitive people."

"Well, that's the last village on this coast that I'm going to visit, and as it's my birthday I feel that somebody ought to take my wishes into consideration," said Mother.

"But of course, Muzzer dear," said Max. "Ve vill now find you a nice place to eat."

The anchor was pulled in, the engine was started, and above the reverberating chug-chug-chug of the engine we could hear the villagers shouting good wishes and clapping as we headed on our way down the coast.

At lunch time we found an enchanting long beach of soft white sand and, as Taki had put his lines out the previous evening and caught some *kefalia*, Spiro built a charcoal fire on the beach and grilled these delicious fish.

Sven, Donald, and Max, still worried by the fact that they had nothing concrete to give Mother for her birthday, concocted a sort of entertainment for her. Sven, who was a sculptor, constructed an enormous nude woman out of damp sand, which Mother was forced to admire, and he then played his accordion for her, fortunately not Bach but some gay and sprightly tunes.

Donald and Max went into a huddle and presently they consulted in a secretive manner with Sven, who nodded his head vigorously.

"We're now," said Donald to Mother, "going to dance an old Austrian dance for you."

This, from the incredibly British and normally introvert Donald, came as such a surprise that even Larry was speechless. Sven crashed into an exceedingly vivid piece of music which was not unlike a mazurka, and the tall and gangling Max and the medium-sized, pale-faced Donald solemnly bowed to each other and then, holding hands, proceeded to dance. To our astonishment they did it remarkably well, prancing and twirling on the sand, with complicated movements in which they had to slap each other's knees and hands and then leap in the air and slap their legs, and other intricate maneuvers of this sort. They reminded me irresistibly of the Gryphon and the Mock Turtle dancing the Lobster Quadrille in *Alice in Wonderland*. So good was their dance that when they came to the end we all spontaneously burst out clapping, whereupon, beaming and perspiring profusely, they gave us an encore with a different tune.

After our *corps de ballet* had had a swim to cool off, we all lay on the sand and ate delicious, succulent fish with the lovely smoky, charcoaly flavor on their charred skins, and rounded off the meal with a variety of fruits.

"Well, that really was a lovely birthday lunch," said Mother. "I did enjoy it. And Sven's playing and Donald and Max's dancing made it absolutely complete."

"Ve'll have a birzday dinner," said Max. "Let's go on to anozzer beach and have a birzday dinner."

So once again we got ourselves on the boat and headed off down the coast. The sun was just setting and the sky was beautifully smeared with red and green and gold when we came to what seemed to be the ideal spot. It was a tiny, rounded bay with a small beach surrounded by towering cliffs which glowed almost tangerine orange in the setting sun's light.

"Oh, this is beautiful," said Mother.

"Here ve'll have de birzday dinner," said Max.

Spiro told Taki that we would make this our landfall for the night. It was unfortunate, however, that it was a bay Taki had never been into before and he did not know that across one part of it was a sand bar. He nosed the benzina into the bay at a fair speed and so was upon the sand bar before he realized it. We came to a sudden and shuddering halt. At that precise moment Mother was standing in the stern admiring the sunset and so the boat's sudden halt threw her off balance and she fell overboard. Now, although she did occasionally deign to lie in shallow water in very hot weather, she could not swim. This everybody, with the exception of Taki, knew. So in unison the entire company leapt overboard to rescue her – including Spiro, who simply adored Mother but who couldn't swim either. The result was complete and utter chaos.

Donald and Max dived on top of each other and banged their heads together. Leonora, in diving, caught her foot on the side of the boat and gave it a nasty gash. Margo, under the impression that Mother was under the water instead of on top of it, dived deep and searched frantically for her body until her breath ran out and she was forced to surface. It was Leslie and Mactavish who seized Mother, for Larry had suddenly realized that Spiro could not swim and he was going down for the third time when Larry rescued him. But all the time he was sinking and rising in the water, Spiro was shouting, "Don'ts you worrys, Mrs. Durrells, don'ts you worrys!" in between spitting out great mouthfuls of seawater.

Leslie and Mactavish towed the panting, spluttering Mother to the shallow water of the sand bar, where she could sit and cough up the seawater she had imbibed so freely, and Larry towed Spiro there so that he could do the same. Then, when they had recovered sufficiently, we got them back on board and had to give Mother a stiff brandy so she could recover from the shock of falling into the water and to give Spiro another so he could recover from the shock of seeing Mother fall.

"Gollys, Mrs. Durrells," he said, "I thoughts you'd be drowns."

"I thought exactly the same thing," said Mother. "I don't think I've ever been in such deep water in my life."

"Neithers have I," said Spiro seriously.

With the united efforts of us all pushing from the sand bar and Taki putting the engine into reverse, we got the benzina free and Taki, having examined the lay of the land, turned it slightly and we got into the bay without any further difficulty.

We lit a fire on the beach and ate octopus and tiny cuttlefish from the ice-box and followed this up with cold chicken and fruit.

"You see what a good idea it was," said Larry, stuffing a great tentacle of octopus into his mouth, "to bring the ice-box."

"Yes, dear," said Mother. "I didn't think it was a good idea at the time, but it has turned out to be very successful, although of course the ice is melting much more quickly on board the boat than it would do in the villa."

"Oh, it's bound to," said Larry. "Still, it'll see us out."

That night the moon was so beautiful that we all lay in the shallow warm water and drank and talked. It couldn't have been more peaceful, when suddenly the air reverberated and the cliffs echoed with a series of pistol shots.

Unbeknownst to us, Leslie and Mactavish had taken Mother's pearl-handled revolver to the farther end of the bay, where Mactavish was showing Leslie how rapidly you learned to fire when you were in the Royal Canadian Mounted Police.

"God almighty!" said Larry. "What the hell do they think they're doing? Turning the bay into a rifle range at Bisley?"

"Gollys," said Spiro, "I thoughts it was thems son-of-a-bitch Turks."

"Leslie dear," shouted Mother, "do please stop doing that."

"We're only practicing," Leslie shouted back.

"Yes, but you've no idea how much noise it's making here," said Mother. "It's echoing back from these cliffs and giving me a headache."

"Oh, all right," said Leslie, disgruntled.

"That's the trouble with Leslie," said Larry. "He's not esthetic. Here's a beautiful, warm sea and nice wine and a full moon, and what does he do? He rushes around firing off revolvers!"

"Well, you do things that annoy us," said Margo indignantly.

"What have I done to annoy you?" asked Larry. "Nothing at all. I'm far and away the sanest member of this family."

"You're about as sane as a . . . as a lunatic," said Margo.

"Now, now, dears, don't quarrel," said Mother; "you know it's my birthday."

"I will play for you," said Sven, and he played a series of melodies which were soft and beautiful, even coming from an accordion, and they fitted the mood and the setting very well.

Presently we brought our mattresses ashore, spread them along the beach and, one by one, dropped off to sleep.

After breakfast the next morning we had a quick swim and got on board the boat. The anchor was pulled up and Taki started the engine. It coughed into life, we moved some six inches, and then the engine died.

"Oh, God, don't tell me we're going to have engine trouble," said Larry.

Spiro, scowling, went to consult with Taki. We heard them muttering together and then suddenly Spiro's voice, like the roar of a bull, raised in anger, heaping obscenities upon Taki's head.

"What the hell's the matter?" asked Larry.

"This stupids bastards," said Spiro, red with rage, pointing a stubby, quivering finger at Taki. "This stupids bastards – if you will excuses this words, Mrs. Durrells – forgot to gets any more petrols."

"Why did he forget?" we all asked in unison.

"He says he meants to, but he forgot when he hads to go and gets the ice-boxes."

"There you are!" said Mother. "I knew it! I *knew* you shouldn't have moved that ice-box!"

"Now don't start on that again," said Larry. "Where's the next place we can get petrol from?"

"Taki says it's Metaloura," said Spiro.

"Well, that's simple enough," said Mactavish. "We can row there in the dinghy."

"I don't know whether it's escaped your notice or not," said Donald, "but we have no dinghy."

It was very curious that none of us had noticed this, for most benzinas, especially on a trip of this sort, trailed a small boat behind them.

"Well," said Mactavish, flexing his muscles, "I'm as fit as a fiddle. I can swim there and get help."

"No, Mr. Mactavish," said Spiro glumly, "it's ten kilometers."

"Well, I can land on beaches and things and have a rest," said Mactavish. "Easily do it by nightfall. Be back in the morning."

Spiro scowled thoughtfully and then turned to Taki and translated Mactavish's idea to him. But Taki was vehement. As from this bay to the next bay where petrol could be obtained it was practically all sheer cliffs, there would be nowhere one could go ashore for a rest.

"Oh dear," said Mother, "what are we going to do?"

"Well, just sit here," said Larry. "It's quite simple."

"What do you mean, it's quite simple?" asked Mother.

"Well, we just sit here and when a boat passes we signal it, and it will then go down the coast and bring us some petrol. I don't know what you're all getting so fussed about."

"Master Larry's rights, Mrs. Durrells," said Spiro dismally. "We can'ts do anythings else."

"Anyway, it's a delightful spot," said Larry. "I mean, if we *had* to break down we couldn't have chosen a better place."

So we all got off the boat and sat about on the beach, leaving Taki sitting cross-legged in the bows of our immobilized craft, keeping a careful eye on the mouth of the bay for any fishing boat that could come to our rescue.

The day passed pleasantly enough but no fishing boat passed, and by nightfall Mother was getting increasingly agitated.

"I do wish you'd stop fussing, Mother," said Larry. "There's sure to be one tomorrow, and we've got plenty of supplies."

"That's just the point," said Mother; "we *haven't* got plenty of supplies. I didn't bring enough to allow for a break-down, and in any case the ice is melting so fast that if we don't get a boat tomorrow half the food will go bad."

This was an aspect of our predicament which had not until then struck us. The little bay with its towering cliffs provided none of the amenities that Robinson Crusoe had found on his island. There was a tiny spring of fresh water that trickled down the face of the cliff and formed a stagnant pool in which Theodore had discovered so many forms of life that none of us felt it would be suitable for drinking should our supply of liquid run out.

"Muzzer is not to worry," said Max, throwing his

arms around her protectively. "If necessary ve vill all get behind de boat and push her back to Corfu."

"Damned silly suggestion," said Donald. "Just the sort of suggestion a Continental would make. God knows how many tons she weighs. Couldn't possibly push her."

"I'm afraid Donald's quite right," said Mactavish. "Fit though I am for my age, I feel that even all of us together couldn't get her very far."

"I do wish you'd stop carrying on like this," said Larry irritably; "after all, this whole coast is littered with fishing boats. There's bound to be one along tomorrow."

"Well, I hope you're right," said Mother. "Otherwise I'm going to have to ration the food."

"Also, I know it's only a minor point, but some of these specimens I've got are quite rare," said Theodore, "and unless I can get them back to Corfu fairly soon, I'm afraid . . . you know . . . because they are so fragile, they are . . . you know . . . going to disintegrate."

We all went to bed in an uneasy frame of mind and Taki and Spiro took it in turns to sit in the bows of the benzina watching in case one of the night fishermen passed whom they could spot by his carbon light. But dawn came and still there was no sign of rescue. To add to our plight, the ice was melting at an alarming rate and we had to dig a hole in the sand and bury quite a lot of the more delicate and perishable foodstuffs that Mother had brought. We had a very meagre lunch.

"Oh dear," said Mother, "I do wish we hadn't come."

"Do not worry, Muzzer," said Max; "help is on de way. I feel it in my bones."

"I think Larry's right," said Donald. "Lots of fishing boats along this stretch of coast. One's bound to come along sooner or later."

"Well, it had better be sooner than later," said Mother, "otherwise we're all going to starve to death."

"It's all Larry's fault," said Leslie belligerently, for he was feeling hungry. "He suggested the trip."

"Now, don't turn on me," said Larry angrily. "You were just as much in favor of it as I was. If the damned thing had been organized properly we wouldn't be in this predicament."

"I agree with Leslie," said Margo. "It was Larry's suggestion."

"I didn't suggest we run out of petrol in a remote bay surrounded by unclimbable cliffs ten kilometres away from the nearest source of supplies," said Larry.

"Now, now, dears," said Mother, "don't quarrel. There'll be a fishing boat along soon."

"In the meantime," said Sven, "I will play to you, my dear Mrs. Durrell, to soothe you."

Unfortunately he chose Bach since, as it apparently soothed him, he was under the impression it soothed everybody else.

But the day passed and no fishing boat appeared. The ice was melting away with great rapidity, and our meal that night would have prompted any Oliver Twist to ask for more.

"Bloody silly," said Larry. "All these damned fishing boats dashing up and down the coast. Why the hell don't they fish in this area?"

"Maybe there'll be a night fisherman tonight," said Mactavish.

Though Spiro and Taki kept watch, nothing passed the mouth of the bay. For breakfast we had a rather soggy peach each. Lunch consisted entirely of watermelons and bread.

"What supplies do we have now?" asked Larry when we had consumed this repast.

"It's rather fortunate that I am a small eater," said Theodore, adding hastily, "I mean, fortunate for me, that is."

"If this goes on I don't know what we're going to do," said Mother, who by now had worked herself into a near panic in spite of everything everybody was trying to do to reassure her.

"Resort to cannibalism," said Larry.

"Larry dear, don't joke like that," said Mother. "It's not funny."

"In any case, ha ha," said Mactavish, "you'd find me rather tough."

"Oh, we'd start on you," said Larry, fixing him with a baleful stare. "We'd have you as a rather indigestible hors d'œuvre. But Leonora, cooked slowly in the sand as they do it in Polynesia, would, I feel, be absolutely delicious. Toes, buttocks, and breast."

"Larry, don't be disgusting," said Margo. "I couldn't possibly eat a human being."

"Damned bad form," said Donald. "Only wogs eat each other."

"It's surprising, though, what you can do when you have to," said Theodore. "I think it was in Bosnia where several villages were snowed up for an unprecedented number of months and, er . . . quite a few of the villagers took to cannibalism."

"Now, will you all stop talking about cannibalism," said Mother. "You'll only make matters worse."

"Well, you still haven't answered my question," said Larry. "What are our supplies at the moment?"

"Watermelons," said Mother, "three green peppers,

and two loaves of bread. Taki is trying to catch some fish but he says it isn't a very good bay for fish."

"But surely there were a couple of legs of lamb left," said Larry.

"Yes, dear," said Mother, "but the ice has melted to such an extent that they've gone off and so I had to bury them."

"Dear God," said Larry, "it'll have to be cannibalism."

The day passed and still no boat appeared. That evening we had very dried-up bread, slightly shriveled green peppers, and watermelon.

Taki and Spiro took up their watch in the bows of the benzina and we all went to bed feeling extremely hungry.

No boat was sighted during the night. The following morning our situation, from being slightly comic, was becoming quite serious. We were all aboard the benzina holding a council of war. My suggestion that we could exist for another couple of days by eating limpets was immediately crushed underfoot.

"My specimens, you know, are deteriorating quite fast," said Theodore in a worried tone of voice.

"Oh, damn your bloody specimens," said Larry. "If only you'd collect something more substantial than microscopic life it would help keep us alive now."

"I really don't know what we're going to do," said Mother.

We had one minute portion of bread each for breakfast and that was the end of our supplies.

"I suppose we'll all just die here," she went on, "and it's not the sort of place that I would choose to be buried in."

"Muzzer vill not die," said Max affectionately. "If necessary, I vill commit suicide and you can eat me."

Mother was rather taken aback by this lavish offer. "It's awfully kind of you, Max," she said, "but I do hope that won't be necessary."

Just at that precise moment Spiro, who had been standing in the bows of the boat, uttered one of his bull roars that made the cliffs echo and bounce.

"Here! Here!"

He was shouting and waving his arms and we saw a small boat with a tiny, rather decrepit engine attached to it passing across the mouth of the bay.

"Here! Here!" shouted Spiro again, in Greek. "Come here!"

So rich and deep was Spiro's voice and such tremendous lung power lay in his stocky frame that, aided by the echo chamber of the cliffs that surrounded us, he actually made the man in the boat hear him. The man turned and looked in our direction. We all rushed to the bows of the boat and made wild gestures beckoning him to come to us. He switched off his engine and Spiro bellowed once more, "Come here! Come here!"

"Who, me?" called the man in the fishing boat.

"But of course *you*," said Spiro. "Who else?"

"You want *me* to come to *you*?" asked the man in the boat, getting things quite clear in his mind.

Spiro called upon Saint Spiridion and several other local saints.

"But of course YOU!" he roared. "Who else is there?"

The man looked around him carefully.

"Nobody," he called back.

"Well, it's *you* that I want then," shouted Spiro.

"What do you want?" inquired the man interestedly.

"If you come closer I can tell you," yelled Spiro, muttering to himself, "idiot!"

"All right," said the man.

He switched on his engine and came zig-zagging towards us.

"Thank God," said Mother in a trembling voice, "oh, thank God."

I must say that at that juncture we all shared her feelings.

The little boat, some twelve feet long, came nosing up to us and the man switched his engine off and bumped gently against our side. He was as brown as a hazel nut, with enormous bluey-black eyes and a curly mop of hair, and it was quite obvious from the very beginning that if he wasn't an idiot he was very close to being one.

He grinned up at the assembled company ingratiatingly.

"*Kalimera,*" he said.

With infinite relief in our voices we all said *kalimera* back.

"Now, listen," said Spiro, taking charge of the situation, "we have. . . ."

"You are Greek?" asked the fisherman, looking at Spiro with interest.

"Of course I'm Greek," shouted Spiro, "but the thing is that. . . ."

"Are all of you Greek?" inquired the fisherman.

"No, no," said Spiro impatiently, "they're foreigners. But the point is that. . . ."

"Oh, foreigners," said the fisherman. "I like foreigners."

He delicately shifted off his foot a dead octopus which had somehow bounced on to it when he had come alongside.

"Would they like to buy fish?" he inquired.

"We don't want to buy fish," roared Spiro.

"But foreigners like fish," the fisherman pointed out.

"Fool!" roared Spiro, tried beyond endurance. "We don't want fish. We want petrol."

"Petrol?" said the fisherman in surprise. "But what do you want petrol for?"

"For this boat," roared Spiro.

"I'm afraid I haven't got enough for that," said the fisherman, glancing at his tiny petrol tin in the bows of his boat. "Tell me, where do they come from?"

"They're English," said Spiro, "but now listen. What I want. . . ."

"The English are a good people," said the fisherman. "There was one only the other day . . . bought two kilos of fish off me and I charged him double and he didn't notice."

"Look!" said Spiro, "what we want is petrol and what I want you to do. . . ."

"Is it a family?" the fisherman inquired.

"No, it's not a family," said Spiro, "but what I want you to do. . . ."

"It *looks* like a family," said the fisherman.

"Well, it's not," said Spiro.

"But he and she look like the mama and the papa," said the fisherman, pointing at Sven and Mother, "and the rest look just like their children. The one with the beard, I suppose, must be the grandfather. What part of England do they come from?"

It was quite obvious that if this went on much longer Spiro would seize an empty wine bottle and bash the fisherman over the head with it.

"Do you think perhaps I ought to have a few words with him?" said Mactavish.

"No," said Larry. "Here, Spiro, let me deal with him." He leaned over the side of the benzina and in his most mellifluous voice said in Greek, "Listen, my soul, we are an English family."

"Welcome," said the fisherman, smiling broadly.

"We have come here in this boat," said Larry slowly and clearly, "and we have run out of petrol. Also we have run out of food."

"Run out of petrol?" said the fisherman. "But you can't move if you haven't got petrol."

"That is exactly the point," said Larry. "So would you be kind enough to let us hire your boat so that we may go down to Metaloura, get some petrol, and bring it back here?"

The fisherman absorbed this information, wiggling his brown toes in the pile of red mullet, squid, and octopus that was lying in the bottom of his boat.

"You will pay me?" he inquired anxiously.

"We will pay you fifty drachmas to take one of us to Metaloura and another fifty drachmas to bring that person back."

Briefly the man's eyes widened with astonishment at this lavish offer.

"You wouldn't give me fifty-five drachmas, would you?" he inquired, but without much hope in his voice, for he realized that the price was a very large sum of money for such a simple task.

"Oh, now, my soul," said Larry, "my golden one, you know I'm offering you a fair price and that I will not cheat you. Would you have it said that you would try and cheat us? You, a Greek, to strangers in your country?"

"Never!" said the fisherman, his eyes flashing, having forgotten the story of the Englishman he had cheated. "A Greek never cheats a foreigner in his country."

"Now, here," said Larry, extracting two fifty-drachma

notes, "is the money. I am giving it to this man who is a Greek like yourself, and he will carry it with him, and when you come back with the petrol I will make sure that he gives it to you without cheating you."

So touched was the fisherman by this that he agreed instantly, and Larry carefully placed the two fifty-drachma notes in the pocket of Spiro's shirt.

"Now, for God's sake, Spiro," he said in English, "get into that bloody boat and go and get us some petrol."

With something of an effort, for he was a portly man, Spiro lowered himself gingerly over the side of the benzina and got into the fisherman's boat, which sank several inches farther into the water.

"Do you want me to go now or this evening?" inquired the fisherman, looking up at Larry.

"*Now!*" said all the Greek-speaking members of the party in unison.

The fisherman started his engine and they headed out into the bay, Spiro sitting like a massive, scowling gargoyle in the bows.

"Oh, I say!" said Donald, as the little boat disappeared round the headland, "how frightfully remiss of us!"

"What's the matter now?" inquired Larry.

"Well, if we had bought all his octopus and fish and things we could have had some lunch," said Donald plaintively.

"By God, you're right," said Larry. "Why didn't you think of it, Mother?"

"I don't see why I should be expected to think of *everything*, dear," she protested. "I thought he was going to tow us down the coast."

"Well, we can always have limpets for lunch," I said.

"If you mention those disgusting things once more, I shall be sick," said Margo.

"Yes, shut up," said Leonora. "We've got enough problems on our hands without you interfering."

So we tried to distract our minds from our empty stomachs. Mactavish gave Leslie lessons in how to draw the pearl-handled revolver rapidly from his hip. Leonora and Margo alternately sun-bathed and swam. Larry, Sven, Donald, and Max argued in a desultory fashion about art and literature. Mother completed some complicated piece of knitting, dropping more than the regulation number of stitches. Theodore, having remarked to everybody's irritation once again that it was a good thing that he was a small eater, pottered off to collect some more specimens in the stagnant pool at the bottom of the cliffs. I took my penknife round to the rocks and fed ravenously on limpets.

Having nothing to eat, we all got rather drunk on the large supply of wine which we still had left, so towards evening Donald and Max were dancing another complicated middle-European dance while Larry was endeavoring to teach Sven to play the "Eton Boating Song" on his accordion. Mother, now secure in her mind at the idea of rescue, had slept peacefully throughout this raucous party, but it got later and later and all of us, although we didn't say anything, had the same thought in mind. Had Spiro, in fact, accompanied by the mad fisherman, reached his destination, or were they marooned as we were in some remote bay? For the fisherman had looked as though his knowledge of navigation was practically nil. As the light was fading, even the effects of the wine did not make us convivial and we sat in a morose cluster, exchanging only an occasional and generally acrimonious remark. It was like the tail end of a good party, when everybody wishes everybody would go home. Even the sky, which had decided to be like burnished copper streaked with gold, elicited no response.

Then, suddenly and unexpectedly, the little fishing boat slid round on the gold-blue water into the bay. There in the stern sat our mad fisherman and there in the bows, like a massive bulldog, sat Spiro. Immediately the complicated and beautiful pattern the sunset had made upon the sea and the sky became twice as vivid. Here was rescue. They had returned!

We gathered in an anxious bunch at the end of the beach as the little boat drew nearer and nearer. Then the fisherman switched off his engine and the boat headed towards us under its own impetus. As the sound of the engine and its echo died away, Spiro shouted in his Minotaurian voice, "Don'ts you worrys, Mrs. Durrells. I've fixed it."

Simultaneously we heaved a sigh of relief, for when Spiro said that he had fixed something we knew it was fixed. The boat came drifting in, nosed and scrunched its way gently onto the sand, and we saw that lying between the fisherman and Spiro was a whole roasted sheep on a spit and beside it a great basket containing all the fruits of the season.

Spiro scrambled clumsily out of the boat and waded massively ashore like some strange sea monster.

"I broughts us foods," he said, "but they hadn't gots any petrols."

"To hell with the petrol," said Larry. "Let's get that food ashore and eat!"

"No, no, Master Larrys, it doesn't matters abouts the petrols," said Spiro.

"But if we haven't got any petrol we're never going to get away from here," said Mother. "And that sheep

57

won't last for long in this heat now that all the ice has melted in the ice-box."

"Don'ts you worrys, Mrs. Durrells," said Spiro. "I tells you I'd fix it and I fixed it. I gots all the fishermens to come down and fetch us."

"What fishermen?" asked Larry. "The only one we've seen is this fugitive from a lunatic asylum."

"No, no, Master Larrys," said Spiro, "I mean the fishermens from Corfus. The ones that comes out at nights."

"I don't know what you're talking about," said Larry.

"I know," I said, eager to display my superior knowledge. "It's a whole fleet of benzinas that come out to fish at night with lights. They fish with nets and lights and I got some of my best specimens from them."

"Did you get those extraordinary *Argonauta argus* from them?" inquired Theodore with interest.

"Yes," I said, "and I also got a duck's-foot starfish."

"Well, I hope to God they're reliable," said Larry.

"I fixed it, Master Larrys," said Spiro in a faintly indignant tone of voice. "They says that they'll be heres at about twos o'clocks."

"After they've finished their fishing, though?" inquired Theodore.

"Yes," said Spiro.

"They might have procured some interesting specimens," said Theodore.

"That's exactly what I thought," I said.

"For God's sake, stop talking about specimens and let's get the food out," said Larry. "I don't know about anybody else but I'm ravenous."

Carefully we extracted the sheep's carcass, burnt and polished by the flames like fumed oak, and the basket of fruit. We transported it to our benzina so that not one morsel of it should be touched with sand, and there we had a most glorious meal.

Now it was night and the moon striped the water orange, yellow, and white. We were replete with food and had drunk far too much wine. Sven played his accordion incessantly while the rest of us all endeavored to do polkas and waltzes and complicated Austrian dances suggested by Max. So vigorously did we dance that Leonora fell over the side in a chrysanthemum-burst of phosphorescence.

Then at two o'clock the fishing fleet arrived and stationed itself, lights gleaming like a string of white pearls, across the mouth of our bay. One benzina detached itself and came chugging in and, after the normal amount of Greek altercation, which made the cliffs echo and tremble, we were hitched up to it, towed away, and joined on to the main fleet.

The fleet started heading for Corfu and, with their lights burning, it seemed to me that we were like the tail end of a comet shooting across the dark waters of space.

As our pilot boat nosed us in gently to the jetty beneath the old fort, Mother said with infinite feeling, "Well, it has been enjoyable in a way, but I'm so glad it's over."

At that precise moment about sixteen drunken fishermen, who had entered into the spirit of the affair as only Greeks can do, were, under Spiro's instructions, moving the ice-box from our benzina onto the jetty. Since they could not move it one way, after some discussion they all turned round and moved it the other way, with the result that half the fishermen and the ice-box dropped into about two fathoms of water.

"You see!" said Mother. "It's the last straw! I *knew* we shouldn't have brought that ice-box.

"Nonsense," said Larry. "Tomorrow morning we can get it out of there as easily as anything."

"But without the ice-box what am I going to *do?*" exclaimed Mother. "I'll have to reorganize *all* the food for at least three or four days."

"Oh, do stop fussing," said Larry. "Really, one would think it was a major catastrophe. Spiro can bring the food up to us."

"Well, it may not be a major catastrophe as far as you're concerned," said Mother frigidly, "but it is as far as *I* am concerned."

Having embraced and said farewell to the rest of the party, we got into Spiro's car and he drove us out to the villa. Although Larry hummed merrily and Leslie showed Mother the beauty and intricacies of the pearl-handled revolver, although Margo tried to persuade her that the dress length would be absolutely ideal for her, and even I tried to lighten her spirits by telling her about a rare butterfly I had managed to catch with her birthday butterfly net, Mother maintained a frigid silence until we reached the villa. Obviously the loss of her precious ice-box had wounded her deeply.

When we got in she poured herself a very stiff brandy and sat on the sofa, obviously trying to work out menus that one could cope with without an ice-box until it was retrieved from the depths of the sea, as we all – including Spiro – assured her it would be.

Larry had found some mail waiting for him. Filling a glass with wine, he started to open the letters with interest.

"Oh good!" he exclaimed when he got to the second letter. "The Grubensteins are coming . . . and they're bringing Gertrude with them."

Mother came out of her gastronomic trance.

"Grubensteins?" she said. "You don't mean that greasy little man who looks as though he hasn't washed for six weeks and that awful gipsy-like wife of his?"

"Great talent," said Larry. "He's going to make a fine poet. She paints awfully well. Gertrude's very interesting, too. You'll like her."

"The less I see of them," said Mother with dignity, "the better I'll be pleased. I don't know about this Gertrude woman, but the Grubensteins left a great deal to be desired."

"What d'you mean, the less you see of them?" said Larry with surprise. "They're coming to stay here."

"You haven't invited them *here!*" Mother said, startled.

"Of course I have," said Larry, as though it was the most natural thing in the world; "they've got no money to stay anywhere else."

Mother took a large gulp of brandy, put on her spectacles and what she considered to be her most fierce expression. "Now look here, Larry," she said in a firm tone of voice, "this has got to stop. I will not have you inviting all these people, at least not without letting me know. When are they supposed to be arriving?"

"The day after tomorrow," said Larry.

"Well, it's got to stop," said Mother. "My nerves won't stand it."

"I don't see what you're carping about," said Larry irritably; "they're a very nice trio. And anyway, you've just had a nice holiday, haven't you?"

❦ A Transport of Terrapins ❦

TOWARDS THE END OF 1939, when it looked as though war was inevitable, my family uprooted itself from Corfu and came back to England. We settled for a time in a flat in London while Mother made repeated forays into different parts of the English countryside in search of a house. And while she was doing this I was free to explore London. Although I have never been a lover of big cities, I found London, at that time, fascinating. After all, the biggest metropolis I was used to was the town of Corfu, which was about the size of a small English market town, and so the great sprawling mass of London had hundreds of exciting secrets for me to discover. There was, of course, the Natural History Museum, and the inevitable visits to the zoo, where I got on quite intimate terms with some of the keepers. This only strengthened my belief that working in a zoo was the only real vocation for anyone and strengthened me in my desire to have one of my own.

Quite close to the flat where we were staying was a shop which always had my undivided attention. It was a place called "The Aquarium," and its window was full of great tanks of brightly colored fish and, what was even more interesting, rows of glass-fronted boxes containing grass snakes, pine snakes, great green lizards, and bulbous-eyed toads. I used to gaze longingly in the

A Transport of Terrapins

window at these beautiful creatures and I had a great desire to own them. But as I already had two magpies, a host of other birds, and a marmoset in the flat, I felt that the introduction of further livestock of any shape or form would bring down the wrath of the family upon me, and so I could only gaze longingly at these lovely reptiles.

Then one morning, when I happened to pass the shop, my attention was riveted to a notice leaning up against an aquarium. It said, "Wanted: Young, reliable assistant." I went back to the flat and thought about it for some time.

"They've got a job going in that pet shop down the road," I said to Mother.

"Have they, dear?" she said, not really taking any notice.

"Yes. They say they want a young, reliable assistant. I . . . I thought of applying for it," I said carelessly.

"What a good idea," said Larry. "Then, perhaps, you could take all your animals there."

"I don't think they'd let him do that, dear," said Mother.

"How much do you think they'd pay for a job like that?" I asked.

"Not very much, I shouldn't think," said Larry. "I doubt that you are what they mean by reliable."

"They'd have to pay me something, wouldn't they?" I asked.

"Are you old enough to be employed?" inquired Larry.

"I'm almost sixteen," I said.

"Well, go and have a shot at it," he suggested.

So the following morning I went down to the pet shop and went in. A short, slender, dark man with very large horn-rimmed spectacles danced across the floor towards me.

"Good morning! Good morning! Good morning, sir!" he said. "What can I do for you?"

"You, um . . . you want an assistant. . . ." I said.

He cocked his head on one side and his eyes grew large behind his spectacles.

"An assistant," he said. "Do you mean to say you want the job?"

"Er . . . yes," I said.

"Have you had any experience?" he inquired doubtfully.

"Oh, I've had plenty of experience," I said. "I've always kept reptiles and fish and things like that. I've got a whole flatful of things now."

The little man looked at me.

"How old are you?" he asked.

"Sixteen . . . nearly seventeen," I lied.

"Well," he said, "we can't afford to pay very much, you know. The overheads on this shop are something extraordinary. But I could start you off at one pound ten."

"That's all right," I said. "When do I start?"

"You'd better start on Monday," he said. "I think on Monday because then I can get all your cards stamped up and straight. Otherwise we get in such a muddle, don't we? Now, my name's Mr. Romilly."

I told him my name and we shook hands rather formally, and then we stood looking at each other. It was quite obvious that Mr. Romilly had never employed anyone before and didn't know quite what the form was. I thought perhaps I ought to help him out.

"Perhaps you could just show me round," I suggested, "and tell me a few things that you will want me to do."

"Oh, what an excellent idea," said Mr. Romilly. "An excellent idea!"

He danced round the shop waving his hands like butterfly wings and showed me how to clean out a fish tank, how to drop the mealworms into the cages of frogs and toads, and where the brush and broom were kept for sweeping the floor. Under the shop was a large cellar where various fish foods, nets, and other things were kept, and it included a constantly running tap that dripped into a large bowl containing what at first glance appeared to be a raw sheep's heart. This, on close inspection, turned out to be a closely knitted ball of threadlike tubifex worms. These bright red worms were a favorite food of all the fish and some of the amphibians and reptiles as well. I discovered that in addition to the delightful things in the window there were hosts of other creatures in the shop – cases full of lizards, toads, tortoises, and treacle – shiny snakes, tanks of moist, gulping frogs, and newts with frilled tails like pennants. After having spent so many months in dry, dusty, desiccated London, I found the shop a Garden of Eden.

"Now," said Mr. Romilly, when he had shown me everything, "you start on Monday, hm? Nine o'clock sharp. Don't be late, will you?"

Nothing short of death would have prevented me from being there at nine o'clock on Monday.

So at ten to nine on Monday morning I paced the pavement outside the shop until eventually Mr. Romilly appeared, clad in a long black coat and a black Homburg hat, waving his bunch of keys musically.

"Good morning, good morning," he trilled. "I'm glad to see you're on time. What a good start."

So we went into the shop and I started on the first

chores of the day, which were to sweep the already almost spotless floor clean and then to go round feeding little knots of wriggling tubifex to the fish.

I very soon discovered that Mr. Romilly, though a kindly man, had little or no knowledge of the creatures in his care. Most of the cages were most unsuitably decorated for the occupants' comfort and, indeed, so were the fish tanks. Also, Mr. Romilly worked on the theory that if you got an animal to eat one thing, you then went on feeding it that incessantly. I decided that I would have to take a hand both in the cage decoration and also in brightening up the lives of our charges, but I knew I would have to move cautiously, for Mr. Romilly was nothing if not conservative.

"Don't you think the lizards and toads and things would like a change from meal-worms, Mr. Romilly?" I asked one day.

"A change?" said Mr. Romilly, his eyes widening behind his spectacles. "What sort of a change?"

"Well," I said, "how about wood lice? I always used to feed my reptiles on wood lice."

"Are you sure?" asked Mr. Romilly.

"Quite sure," I said.

"It won't do them any harm, will it?" he asked anxiously.

"No," I said, "they love wood lice. It gives them a bit of variety."

"But where are we going to get them?" asked Mr. Romilly despondently.

"Well, I expect there are plenty in the parks," I said. "I'll see if I can get some, shall I?"

"Very well," said Mr. Romilly reluctantly, "if you're quite sure they won't do them any harm,"

So I spent one afternoon in the park and collected

a very large tin full of wood lice, which I kept in decaying leaves down in the cellar, and when I thought that the frogs and the toads and the lizards had got a bit bored with the meal-worms, I would try them on some meal-worm beetles, and then, when they had had a surfeit of those, I would give them some wood lice. At first, Mr. Romilly used to peer into the cages with a fearful look on his face, as though he expected to see all the reptiles and amphibians dead. But when he found that they not only thrived on this new mixture but even started to croak in their cages, his enthusiasm knew no bounds.

My next little effort concerned two very large and benign leopard toads which came from North Africa. Now, Mr. Romilly's idea of North Africa was an endless desert where the sun shone day and night and where the temperature was never less than a hundred and ninety in the shade, if indeed any shade was to be found. He had therefore incarcerated these two poor toads in a small, glass-fronted cage with a couple of brilliant electric light bulbs above them. They sat on a pile of plain white sand, they had no rocks to hide under to get away from the glare, and the only time the temperature dropped at all was at night when we switched off the lights in the shop. So these poor toads were sitting in a temperature of about a hundred degrees all day long. In consequence, their eyes had become milky and looked almost as though they were suffering from cataracts, their skins had become dry and flaky, and the soles of their feet were raw. I knew that suggesting to Mr. Romilly anything so drastic as putting them into a new cage with some damp moss would horrify him, so I started surreptitiously to try and give the toads a slightly happier existence. I pinched some olive oil from my mother's kitchen for a start, and when Mr. Romilly went out to have his lunch hour, I massaged the oil into the skin of both toads. This improved the flakiness. I then got some ointment from the chemist, having explained – to his amusement – why I wanted it, and anointed their feet with it. This helped, but it did not clear up the foot condition completely. I also got some Golden Eye Ointment, which one normally used for dogs, and applied it to their eyes with miraculous results. Then, every time Mr. Romilly had his lunch hour I would give them a warm spray and this they loved. They would sit there, gulping benignly, blinking their eyes and, if I moved the spray a little, they would shuffle across the floor of their cage to get under it again. One day I put a small section of moss in the cage and both toads immediately burrowed under it.

"Oh, look, Mr. Romilly," I said with well-simulated surprise, "I put a bit of moss in the toads' cage by mistake, and they seem to like it."

"Moss?" said Mr. Romilly. "Moss? But they live in the desert."

"Well, I think some parts of the desert have got a *little* bit of vegetation," I said.

"I thought it was all sand," said Mr. Romilly. "All sand. As far as the eye could see."

"No, er . . . I think they've got some small cactuses and things," I said. "Anyway, they seem to like it, don't they?"

"They certainly do," said Mr. Romilly. "Do you think we ought to leave it in?"

"Yes," I said. "Shall we put a little more in, too?"

"I don't suppose it could do any harm. They can't eat it and strangle themselves with it, can they?" he asked anxiously.

"I don't think they will," I said reassuringly.

So from then onwards my two lovely toads had a bit of moss to hide under and, what was more important, a bed of moss to sit on, and their feet soon cleared up.

I next turned my attention to the fish, for although they loved tubifex dearly, I felt that they too should have a little variety in their diet.

"Wouldn't it be possible," I suggested to Mr. Romilly in a tentative sort of way, "to give the fish some daphnia?"

Now, daphnia are little water fleas, which we used to get from the farm that supplied the shop with all its produce – such as waterweed and water snails and freshwater fish – and sell in little pots to fish lovers to feed to their fish.

"Daphnia?" said Mr. Romilly. "Feed them on daphnia? But they wouldn't eat it, would they?"

"Well, if they won't eat it, why do we sell it to people to feed to their fish?" I inquired.

Mr. Romilly was very powerfully struck by this piece of logic.

"You're right, you know," he said. "You're right. There's a little left over down in the cellar now. The new supply comes tomorrow. Try some on them and see."

So I dropped about a tablespoonful of daphnia into each tank and the fish went as mad over them as the toads and frogs had gone over the wood lice.

The next thing I wanted to do, but I had to do it more cautiously, was to try and decorate the cages and tanks to make them more attractive. Now, this was a task that Mr. Romilly always undertook himself, and he did it with a dogged persistence. I do not think he really enjoyed it, but he felt that, as the senior member of the firm, it was his duty.

"Mr. Romilly," I said one day. "I've got nothing to

do at the moment and there are no customers. You wouldn't let me decorate a fish tank, would you? I'd love to learn how to do them as well as you do."

"Well, now," said Mr. Romilly, blushing. "Well, now. I wouldn't say I was all that good. . . ."

"Oh, I think you do it beautifully," I said. "And I'd like to learn."

"Well, perhaps just a small one," said Mr. Romilly. "And I can give you some tips as you go along. Now, let's see . . . let's see. . . . Yes, now, that tank of mollies over there. They need clearing out. Now, if you can move them to the spare tank, and then empty it and give it a good scrub, and then we'll start from scratch, shall we?"

And so, with the aid of a little net, I moved all the black mollies, as dark and glistening as little olives, out of their tank and into the spare one. Then I emptied their tank and scrubbed it out and called Mr. Romilly.

"Now," he said, "you put some sand at the bottom and . . . um . . . a couple of stones, and then perhaps some, er . . . vallisneria, I would say, probably in that corner there, wouldn't you?"

"Could I just try it on my own?" I asked. "I, er . . . I think I'd learn better that way. And then, when I'm finished you could criticize it and tell me where I've gone wrong."

"Very good idea," said Mr. Romilly. And so he pottered off to do his petty cash and left me in peace.

It was only a small tank but I worked hard on it. I piled up the silver sand in great dunes. I built little cliffs. I planted forests of vallisneria through which the mollies could drift in shoals. Then I filled it carefully with water, and when it was the right temperature I put the mollies back in it and called Mr. Romilly to see my handiwork.

"By Jove!" he said, looking at it. "By Jove!"

He glanced at me and it was almost as though he was disappointed that I had done so well. I could see that I was on dangerous ground.

"Do . . . do you like it?" I inquired.

"It . . . it's remarkable! Remarkable! I can't think how you . . . how you managed it."

"Well, I only managed it by watching *you*, Mr. Romilly," I said. "If it hadn't been for you teaching me, I could never have done it."

"Well, now. Well, now," said Mr. Romilly, going pink. "But I see you've added one or two little touches of your own."

"Well, they were just ideas I'd picked up from watching you," I said.

"Hmmm. . . . Most commendable. Most commendable," said Mr. Romilly.

The next day he asked me whether I would like to decorate another fish tank and I knew that I had won the battle without hurting his feelings.

The tank that I really desperately wanted to do was the enormous one that we had in the window. It was some four and a half feet long and about two feet six deep, and in it we had a great colorful mixed collection of fish. But I knew that I must not overstep the bounds of propriety at this stage. So I did several smaller fish tanks first, and when Mr. Romilly was thoroughly used to the idea of my doing them, I then broached the subject of our big show tank in the window.

"Could I try my hand at that, Mr. Romilly?" I asked.

"What? Our show piece?" he said.

"Yes," I said. "It's . . . it's in need of . . . of a clean, anyway. So I thought, perhaps, I could try redecorating it."

"Well, I don't know. . . ," said Mr. Romilly doubtfully.

"I don't know. It's a most important piece that, you know. It's the centrepiece of the window. It's the one that attracts all the customers."

He was quite right, but the customers were attracted by the flickering shoals of multicolored fish, not by Mr. Romilly's attempts at decoration, which made it look rather like a blasted heath.

"Well, could I just try?" I said. "And if it's no good, I'll do it all over again. I'll even . . . I'll even spend my half day doing it."

"Oh, I'm sure that won't be necessary," said Mr. Romilly, shocked. "You don't want to spend all your days shut up in the shop, you know. A young boy like you . . . you want to be out and about. . . . Well, all right, you try your hand at it, and see what happens."

It took me the better part of a day to do, because in between times I had to attend to the various customers who came to buy tubifex or daphnia or a tree frog for their garden pond. I worked on that giant tank with all the dedication of a marine Capability Brown. I built rolling sand dunes and great towering cliffs of lovely granite. And then, through the valleys between the granite mountains, I planted forests of vallisneria and other, more delicate, weedy ferns. And on the surface of the water I floated the tiny little white flowers that look like miniature water-lilies. With the aid of sand and rocks I concealed the heater, thermostat, and aerator, all of which were rather ugly. When I had finally finished it and replaced the brilliant scarlet sword-tails, the shiny black mollies, the silver hatchet fish, and the brilliant Piccadilly-like neon tetras and stepped back to observe my handiwork, I found myself deeply impressed by my own genius. Mr. Romilly, to my delight, was ecstatic about the whole thing.

A Transport of Terrapins

"Exquisite! Exquisite!" he exclaimed. "Simply exquisite."

"Well, you know what they say, Mr. Romilly," I said. "That a good pupil needs a good master."

"Oh, you flatter me, you flatter me," he said, wagging his finger at me playfully. "This is a case where the pupil has surpassed the master."

After that, I was allowed to decorate all the tanks and all the cages. I think Mr. Romilly was secretly rather relieved not to have to urge his non-existent artistic sense into this irksome task.

After one or two experiments, I always took my lunch hour at a little café not far from the shop. Here I had discovered a kindly waitress who, in exchange for a little flattery, would give me more than the regulation number of sausages with my sausages and mash, and warn me against the deadly perils of the Irish stew on that particular day. One day when I was going to have my lunch, I discovered a short cut to the café. It was a narrow little alleyway that ran between the great groups of shops and the towering houses and flats. It was cobblestoned and as soon as I got into it, it was as though I had been transported back to Dickensian London. I found that part of it was tree-lined and farther along there were a series of tiny shops. It was then that I discovered that we were not the only pet shop in the vicinity, for I came across the abode of Henry Bellow.

The dirty window of his shop measured perhaps six feet square by two deep. It was crammed from top to bottom with small square cages, each containing one or a pair of chaffinches, greenfinches, linnets, canaries, or budgerigars. The floor of the window was inches deep in seed husks and bird excrement, but the cages themselves were spotlessly clean and each sported a

73

bright green sprig of lettuce or groundsel and a white label on which had been written in shaky block letters "SOLD." The glass door of the shop was covered with a yellowed lace curtain, and between it and the glass hung a cardboard notice which said, "Enter Please," in Gothic letters. The reverse side of this notice, I was to learn, stated equally politely, "We regret we are closed." Never, in all the days that I hurried for my sausages and mash up this uneven flagged alley, had I ever seen a customer entering or leaving the shop. Indeed, the shop seemed lifeless except for the occasional lethargic hopping from perch to perch of the birds in the window. I wondered, as the weeks passed, why all the birds in the window were not claimed by the people who had bought them. Surely the various owners of some thirty assorted birds could not have decided simultaneously that they did not want them? And, in the unlikely event of this happening, why had the 'Sold' signs not been removed? It was a mystery that in my limited lunch hour I had little time to investigate. But my chance came one day when Mr. Romilly, who had been dancing round the shop singing "I'm a busy little bee," went down into the basement and suddenly uttered a falsetto screech of horror. I went and peered down the stairs, wondering what I had done or left undone.

"What's the matter, Mr. Romilly?" I asked cautiously.

Mr. Romilly appeared at the foot of the stairs clasping his brow, distraught.

"Stupid *me!*" he intoned. "Stupid, stupid, *stupid* me!"

Gathering from this that I was not the culprit, I took heart.

"What's the matter?" I asked solicitously.

"Tubifex and daphnia!" said Mr. Romilly tragically,

removing his spectacles and starting to polish them feverishly.

"Have we run out?"

"Yes," intoned Mr. Romilly sepulchrally. "How stupid of me! What negligence! How very, very remiss of me. I deserve to be sacked. I really am the stupidest mortal...."

"Can't we get some from somewhere else?" I asked, interrupting Mr. Romilly's verbal flagellation.

"But the farm always sends it up," exclaimed Mr. Romilly, as though I were a stranger in need of an explanation. "The farm always sends up the supply when I ask for it, every weekend. And I, crass idiot that I am, never ordered any."

"But can't we get it from somewhere *else?*" I asked.

"And the guppies and the sword-tails and the black mollies, they so look forward to their tubifex," said Mr. Romilly, working himself into a sort of hysterical self-pity. "They relish it. How can I face those tiny pouting faces against the glass? How can I eat my lunch while those poor little fish...."

"Mr. Romilly," I interrupted firmly. "Can we get some tubifex from somewhere other than the farm?"

"Eh?" said Mr. Romilly, staring at me. "Other than the farm? But the farm always sends.... Ah, wait a bit. I see what you mean.... Yes...."

He climbed laboriously up the wooden stairs, mopping his brow, and emerged like the sole survivor of a pit disaster. He gazed round him with vacant, tragic eyes.

"But where?" he said at last, despairingly. "But where?"

"Well," I said, taking the matter in hand, "what about Bellow?"

"Bellow? Bellow?" he said. "Most unbusinesslike chap. He deals in birds. Shouldn't think he'd have any."

"But surely it's worth a try?" I said. "Let me go round and see."

Mr. Romilly thought about it.

"All right," he said at last, averting his face from the serried ranks of accusing-looking fish, "take ten shillings out of petty cash, and don't be too long."

He handed me the key and sat down, gazing glumly at his highly polished shoes. I opened the tin petty cash box, extracted a ten-shilling note, filled in a slip – "I.O.U. 10/- Tubifex" – and slipped it into the box, locked it, and pushed the key into Mr. Romilly's flaccid hand. A moment later I was out on the broad pavement, weaving through the vacant-eyed throng of shoppers, making my way towards Bellow's shop, while the mountainous red buses thundered past with their gaggle of attendant taxis and cars. I came to the tiny alleyway and turned down it, and immediately peace reigned. The thunder of buses, the clack of feet, the honk and screech of cars became muted, almost beautiful, like the distant roar of the surf. On one side of the alley was a blank soot-blackened wall. On the other, the iron railings which guarded the precious piece of ground which led to the local church. Here had been planted – by someone of worth – a rank of plane trees. They leant over the iron railings, roofing the alley with green, and on their mottled trunks looper caterpillars performed prodigious and complicated walks, humping themselves grimly towards a goal about which even they seemed uncertain. Where the plane trees ended, the shops began. There were no more than six of them, each Lilliputian in dimensions and each one forlornly endeavoring.

A Transport of Terrapins

There was Clymnestra, Modes for Ladies, with a rather extraordinary fur in their window as the *pièce de résistance* – a fur which, with its glass eyes and its tail in its mouth, would have curdled the heart of any anti-vivisectionist. There was the Pixies' Parlour, Light Luncheons, Teas and Snacks; and next door to it, once you had refreshed yourself, was A. Wallet, Tobacconist, whose window consisted entirely of cigarette and pipe advertisements, the predominant one being the Henry Holman Hunt type of placard for Wills Wild Woodbines. I hurried past all these and past William Drover, Estate Agent, with its host of fascinating pale brown pictures of desirable residences, past the shrouded portal, decorated rather severely and somewhat surprisingly by one rose-pink lavatory pan, of Messrs. M. & R. Drumlin, Plumbers, to the end of the row of shops where the faded notice above the door stated simply and unequivocally: Henry Bellow, Aviculturalist. At last, I thought, I had the chance of getting inside the shop and solving, if nothing else, the mystery of the birds with the "Sold" notices on their cages. But as I approached the shop something unprecedented happened. A tall, angular woman in tweeds, wearing a ridiculous Tyrolean hat with a feather, strode purposefully down the alley and, a brief second before me, she grasped the handle of the door marked "Enter please" and swept in, while the bell jangled melodiously. I paused, astonished. It was the first time I had ever seen a customer enter any of the shops in the alley. Then, anxious to see what happened once she had entered the shop, I rushed after her and caught the closing door on the last jangle.

In an almost lightless shop the woman with the Tyrolean hat and I were caught like moths in some dingy spider's web. The melodious chimes of the door, one felt assured, would have someone running to attend the shop. Instead of which there was silence, except for the faint cheeping of the birds in the window and the sudden shuffling of feathers from a cockatoo in the corner, a sound like un-ironed washing being spread out. Having shuffled its feathers to its satisfaction, it put its head on one side and said, "Hullo, hullo, hullo," very softly and with complete lack of interest.

We waited what seemed a long time but what was probably only a few seconds. While we waited my eyes gradually grew accustomed to the gloom. I saw that there was a small counter and behind it shelves of bird seed, cuttlefish, and other accoutrements of the aviculturalist's trade, and in front of it were a number of large sacks containing hemp and rape and millet seed. In one of these perched a white mouse, eating the seeds with all the frantic speed of a nervous person nibbling cheese straws at a cocktail party. I was beginning to wonder whether to open the door and make the bell jangle again, when suddenly a very large and ancient retriever padded its way solemnly through the door at the back of the shop and came forward, wagging its tail. It was followed by a man I took to be Henry Bellow. He was a tall, stout man with a great mop of curly grey hair and a huge bristling moustache, like an untamed gorse bush, that looked as though it were a suitable nesting site for any number of birds. And from under his shaggy eyebrows his tiny little blue eyes stared out, brilliant as periwinkles, through his gold-rimmed spectacles. He moved with a ponderous slowness, rather like a lazy seal. He came forward and gave a little bow.

"Madam," he said, and his voice had the rich accents of Somerset, "Madam, your servant."

A Transport of Terrapins

The Tyrolean hat looked rather alarmed at being addressed in this fashion.

"Oh, er . . . good day," she said.

"What may I get you?" inquired Mr. Bellow.

"Well, actually, I came to get your advice," she said. "Er . . . it's about my young nephew. He's going to be fourteen soon and I want to buy him a bird for his birthday. . . . He's very keen on birds, you know."

"A bird," said Mr. Bellow. "A bird. And what kind of bird, what particular *species* of bird, have you got in mind, madam?"

"Well, I, er . . . I don't really know," said the lady in the Tyrolean hat. "What about a canary?"

"I wouldn't touch canaries at this time of the year," said Mr. Bellow, shaking his head sorrowfully. "I wouldn't touch them myself. And I would be a dishonest man if I sold you a canary, madam."

"Why at this time of year?" asked the lady, obviously impressed.

"It's a very bad time of the year for canaries," said Mr. Bellow. "Bronchial trouble, you know."

'Oh," said the lady. "Well, what about a budgerigar?"

"Now, I wouldn't advise those either, madam. There's a lot of psittacosis around," said Mr. Bellow.

"A lot of what?" inquired the lady.

"Psittacosis, madam. You know, the parrot's disease. Most of the budgerigars have got it at this time of the year. It's fatal to human beings, you know. I had an inspector from the Ministry of Health only the other day, come to check on mine. He said they were sure to get it sooner or later, so I couldn't possibly sell you one of mine."

"Well, what bird would you suggest, then?" asked the woman, getting rather desperate.

"Actually, madam, it's a very, very bad time of the year to sell birds," said Mr. Bellow. "They're all in moult, you see."

"Then you wouldn't advise me to get a bird?" she said. "How about something else, like . . . like a white mouse, or something similar?"

"Ah, well, I'm afraid you'd have to go somewhere else, madam. I'm afraid I don't deal in them," said Mr. Bellow.

"Oh," she said. "Oh. Well, I suppose I can always go to Harrods."

"A very fine emporium, madam," said Mr. Bellow. "A very fine emporium indeed. I am sure they will be able to satisfy your wants."

"Well, thank you so much," she said. "Most kind of you." And she left the shop.

When the door closed Mr. Bellow turned and looked at me.

"Good afternoon," I said.

"Good afternoon, sir," he said. "And what can I have the pleasure of doing for you?"

"Well, actually, I came to see whether you had any tubifex," I said. "I work at the Aquarium and we've run out of tubifex."

"At the Aquarium, eh? With that fellow Romilly?"

"That's right," I said.

"Well, well," said Mr. Bellow. "And what makes you think that I would have tubifex? I deal in birds."

"That's what Mr. Romilly said, but I thought there was just a chance that you might have some, for some reason or other, and so I thought I'd come and see."

"Well, it so happens that you're right," said Mr. Bellow. "Come with me."

He led me through the door at the back of the shop

and into the small and untidy but comfortable sitting room. It was quite obvious, from the look of the chair and sofa covers, that the dog enjoyed them as much as Mr. Bellow did. He led me through the back into a little paved yard where the plane trees from the churchyard hung over, and there was a small pond with a tap dribbling into it, and in the middle of it a plaster cupid standing on a mound of rocks. The pond was full of goldfish and at one end of it was a big jam jar in which was a large lump of tubifex. Mr. Bellow fetched another jar and ladled some of the tubifex out into it. Then he handed it to me.

"That's very kind of you," I said. "How much do I owe you?"

"Oh, you don't pay me for it," said Mr. Bellow. "Don't pay me for it. Take it as a gift."

"But . . . but it's awfully expensive," I said, taken aback.

"Take it as a gift, boy. Take it as a gift," he said.

He led me back into the shop.

"Tell me, Mr. Bellow," I asked, "why are all the birds in your window labelled 'Sold'?"

His sharp little blue eyes fastened on me.

"Because they *are* sold," he said.

"But they've been sold for ages. Ever since I've been coming down this alley. And that's a good two months. Doesn't anybody ever come and claim them?"

"No, I just . . . keep them, well, for them, until they're able to have them. Some of them are building their aviaries, constructing cages, and so forth and so forth," said Mr. Bellow.

"Did you sell them when it was the right time of year?" I asked.

A faint flicker of a smile passed over Mr. Bellow's face.

"Yes, indeed I did," he said.

"Have you got other birds?" I asked.

"Yes, upstairs," he said. "Upstairs."

"If I come back another day when I've got more time, can I see them?"

Mr. Bellow gazed at me thoughtfully and stroked the side of his chin.

"I think that might he arranged," he said, "When would you like to come?"

"Well, Saturday's my half day," I said. "Could I come then? Saturday afternoon?"

"I'm normally closed on a Saturday," said Mr. Bellow. "However, if you'll ring the bell three times, I'll let you in."

"Thank you very much," I said. "And thank you for the tubifex. Mr. Romilly will be very grateful."

"Don't mention it," said Mr. Bellow. "Good day to you."

And I went out and made my way down the alley and back to the shop.

For the next couple of days I thought very deeply on the subject of Mr. Bellow. I did not believe for one moment that the birds in his window were sold, but I could not see the point of having them labelled "Sold." Also, I was more than a little puzzled by his obvious reluctance to sell a bird to the woman in the Tyrolean hat. I determined that on Saturday I would do my best to prise the answer to these secrets from Mr. Bellow himself.

When Saturday came I made my way down the alleyway and arrived at Mr. Bellow's shop sharp at two o'clock. The notice on the door said, "We regret that we are closed." Nevertheless I pressed the bell three times and waited hopefully. Presently Mr. Bellow opened the door.

A Transport of Terrapins

"Ah," he said, "good afternoon to you."

"Good afternoon, Mr. Bellow," I said.

"Do come in," he said hospitably.

I went in and he locked the shop door carefully after me.

"Now," he said, "you wanted to see some birds?"

"Yes, please," I said.

He took me out through his living room and up a very tiny rickety staircase. The top part of the shop consisted, as far as I could see, of a minute bathroom, a bedroom, and another room which Mr. Bellow ushered me into. It was lined from floor to ceiling with cages full of birds of all shapes, sizes, colors, and descriptions. There were groups of the tiny vivid little seed-eaters from Africa and Asia. There were even one or two of the gorgeous Australian finches. There were parakeets, green as leaves, and red cardinals that were as crimson as royal robes. I was fascinated. Mr. Bellow proved to be much abler at his job than Mr. Romilly, for he knew the name of each and every bird and its scientific name as well, where it came from, what its food preferences were, and how many eggs it laid. He was a mine of information.

"Are all these birds for sale?" I asked, fixing my eyes greedily on a red cardinal.

"Of course," said Mr. Bellow, and then added, "But only at the right time of year."

"What's all this about the right time of year?" I asked, puzzled. "Surely if you're selling birds you can sell them at any time of the year?"

"Well, some people do," said Mr. Bellow, "But I have always made it a rule never to sell at the wrong time of the year."

I looked at him and I saw that his eyes were twinkling.

"Then when is the right time of the year?" I asked.

"There is never a right time of year as far as I am concerned," said Mr. Bellow.

"You mean you don't sell them at all?" I asked.

"Very rarely," said Mr. Bellow. "Only occasionally, perhaps to a friend."

"Is that why you wouldn't let that woman have a bird the other day?'

"Yes," he said.

"And all those birds in the window marked 'Sold,' they aren't really sold, are they?"

Mr. Bellow gazed at me, judging whether or not I could keep a secret.

"Actually, between you and me, they are not sold," he admitted.

"Well, then how do you make a profit?" I asked.

"Ah," said Mr. Bellow, "that's the point. I don't."

I must have looked utterly bewildered by this news for Mr. Bellow gave a throaty chuckle and said, "Let's go downstairs and have some tea, shall we? And I'll explain it to you. But you must promise that it will go no further. You promise, now?"

He held up a fat finger and waved it at me.

"Oh, I promise!" I said. "I promise."

"Right," he said. "Do you like crumpets?"

"Er . . . yes, I do," I said, slightly bewildered by this change of subject.

"So do I," said Mr. Bellow, "Hot buttered crumpets and tea. Come. . . . Come downstairs,"

And so we went down to the little living room, where Mr. Bellow's retriever, whose name, I discovered, was Aldrich, lay stretched, sublimely comfortable, across the sofa. Mr. Bellow lit a little gas ring and toasted crumpets over it and then buttered them thickly, and when he had made a tottering, oozing pile of them, he placed them on a little table between us. By this time the kettle was boiling and he made the tea and set out thin and delicate china cups for us to drink out of.

We sipped our tea and then he handed me a crumpet, took one himself and sank his teeth into it with a sigh of satisfaction.

"What . . . what were you going to tell me about not making a profit?" I asked.

"Well," he said, wiping his hands and his mouth and his moustache fastidiously with his handkerchief, "it's rather a long and complicated story. The whole of this lane – it's called Potts Lane, by the by – once belonged to an eccentric millionaire called Potts. He was what would be known nowadays, I suppose, as a socialist. When he built this line of shops he laid down special rules and regulations governing them. The people who wanted the shops could have them on an indefinite lease and every four years their rent would come up for revision. If they were doing well, their rent was raised accordingly; if they were not doing so well, their rent was adjusted the opposite way. Now, I moved into this shop in 1921. Since then I have been paying five shillings a week rent."

I stared at Mr. Bellow disbelievingly.

"Five shillings a week?" I said. "But that's ridiculous for a shop like this. Why, you're only a stone's throw away from Kensington High Street."

"Exactly," said Mr. Bellow. "That is exactly the point. I pay five shillings a week, that is to say one pound a month rent."

"But why is the rent so ridiculously small?" I asked.

"Because," he said, "I make no profit. As soon as I discovered this section in the lease I immediately saw that it would provide me with a convenient loop-hole.

I had a little money put by – not very much, but enough to get along on. And what I really wanted was a place to live where I could keep my birds. Well, this provided me with the ideal opportunity. I went round to see all the other people in Potts Lane and explained about this clause to them, and I found that most of them were in a similar predicament as myself; that they had small amounts of money to live on, but what they really wanted was a cheap abode. So we formed the Potts Lane Association and we clubbed together and we got ourselves a very good accountant. When I say 'good' I don't mean one of these wishy-washy fellows who are always on the side of the law; those are no good to man nor beast. No, this is a very sharp, bright young man. And so we meet once every six months or so and he examines our books and tells us how to run at a loss. We run at a loss, and then when our rents come up for revision they either remain static or are slightly lowered."

"But can't the people who own the property now change the leases?" I asked.

"No," said Mr. Bellow, "that is the beauty of it. I found out that by the terms of Mr. Potts' will these conditions have to stand."

"But they must have been furious when they found out that you were only paying them a pound a month?"

"They were indeed," said Mr. Bellow. "They did their very best to evict me, but it was impossible. I got a good lawyer – again, not one of the wishy-washy sort that thinks more of the law than he does of his customers – and he soon put them in their place. They met with an equally united front from all the other shops in the lane, so there was really nothing they could do."

I did not like to say anything because I did not want to hurt Mr. Bellow's feelings, but I felt sure that this

86

story was a complete make-up. I had once had a tutor who lived a sort of schizophrenic existence and would tell me long and complicated stories about adventures that had never happened to him but which he wished had. So I was quite used to this form of prevarication.

"Well, I think it's fascinating," I said. "I think it was awfully clever of you to find it out."

"One should always read the small print," said Mr. Bellow, wagging a finger at me. "Excuse me, but I must go and get Mabel."

He went off into the shop and reappeared with the cockatoo on his wrist. He sat down and, taking the bird in his hands, laid it on its back. It lay there as though carved out of ivory, quite still, its eyes closed, saying "Hullo, hullo, hullo." He smoothed its feathers gently and then placed it on his lap, where he tickled the feathers over its tummy. It lay there drowsing in ecstasy.

"She gets a bit lonely if I keep her out in the shop too long," he explained. "Have another crumpet, my dear boy?"

So we sat and ate crumpets and chatted. Mr. Bellow I found a fascinating companion. In his youth he had travelled quite widely round the world and knew a lot of places intimately that I longed to visit.

After that I used to go and have tea with him about once a fortnight, and they were always very happy afternoons for me.

I was still disbelieving about his story of Potts Lane, so I thought I would conduct an experiment. Over a period of days I visited in turn each shop in the lane. When I went to Clymnestra's, for example, I went to buy a hat for my mother's birthday. They were terribly sorry, said the two dear old ladies who ran it, terribly sorry indeed; I couldn't have come at a worse time. They had

just run out of hats. Well, had they got anything else,
I inquired? A fur, or something? Well, no, as a matter
of fact, they said, all the stuff they had in the shop was
bespoken at the moment. They were waiting for a new
consignment to come in. When was my mother's birthday? Friday week, I said. Oh, we think it will be in by
then, they said; yes, we're sure it will be in by then. Do
come again.

Mr. Wallet, the tobacconist, told me that he did not
stock the brand of cigarettes I wanted. He also did
not stock any cigars, nor did he stock any pipes. Reluctantly, he let me buy a box of matches.

I next went to the plumbers. I had called, I said, on
behalf of my mother because there was something
wrong with our cistern and could they send a man
round to look at it?

"Well, now," said Mr. Drumlin, "how urgent is it?"

"Oh, it's quite urgent," I said. "We're not getting any
water into the lavatories or anything."

"Well, you see, we've only got one man here," he said.
"Only one man and *he's* out on a job . . . quite a *big* job.
Don't know how long it will take him. . . . Maybe a day
or two."

"Couldn't he come round and do a bit of overtime?"
I asked.

"Oh, I don't think he'd like to do that," said Mr.
Drumlin. "There's a very good plumber in the High
Street, though. You could go to them. They might have
a man free. But I'm afraid I couldn't guarantee anything,
not for . . . oh, two or three days – at the *earliest*, that
is, at the *earliest*."

Thanking him, I left. I next went to William Drover,
the estate agent. He was a seedy little man with glasses
and wispy hair like thistledown. I explained that my

aunt was thinking of moving to this part of London and had asked me, since I lived in the vicinity, if I would go to an estate agent and find out about flats for her.

"Flats? Flats?" said Mr. Drover, pursing his lips. He took off his glasses and polished them, replaced them and peered round the shop as though expecting to find a flat hidden there.

"It's an awkward time for flats," he said, "a very awkward time. Lots of people moving into the district, you know. Most of them are snapped up before you have a chance."

"So you've got nothing on your books? No details that I could show to my aunt?" I said.

"No," he said, "nothing at all. Nothing at all, I'm afraid. Nothing at all."

"Well, how about a small house, then?" I asked.

"Ah, they're just as bad. Just as bad," he said. "I don't think I have a single small house on my books that would suit you. I've got a ten-bedroomed house in Hampstead, if that's any use?"

"No, I think that would be a bit big," I said. "In any case, she wants to live in this area."

"They all do. They all do. We're getting crowded out. We'll be standing shoulder to shoulder," he said.

"Surely that's good for business?" I inquired.

"Well, it is and it isn't," he said. "You get overcrowded and the tone of the neighborhood goes down, you know."

"Well, thank you very much for your help, anyway," I said.

"Not at all. Not at all. Sorry I couldn't help you more," he said.

I next went to the Pixies' Parlour. They had quite an extensive menu but all they could offer me was a cup of tea. Most unfortunately – and they were terribly apologetic about it – their van, carrying all their supplies for the day, had broken down somewhere in North London and they were bereft of food of any description.

After this I believed Mr. Bellow's story about Potts Lane.

It was at about this time that another rather strange character appeared in my life. I had now been working for some time with Mr. Romilly and he trusted me implicitly. Periodically he would send me down to the East End of London to collect fresh supplies of reptiles and amphibians and tropical fish. These we got from the wholesalers, whereas the farm (which really ran the shop) sent us all the freshwater stuff that we needed. I enjoyed these jaunts to gloomy, cavernous stores in back streets, where I would find great crates of lizards, basketfuls of tortoises, and dripping tanks, green with algæ, full of newts and frogs and salamanders. It was on one of these forays into the East End that I met Colonel Anstruther.

I had been sent down to Van den Goths, a big wholesaler who specialized in importing North American reptiles and amphibians, and I had been given instructions by Mr. Romilly to bring back a hundred and fifty baby painted terrapins – those enchanting little freshwater tortoises with green shells and yellow and red markings on their skins. They were each about the size of a half-crown. We did quite a brisk trade in these for they were a good and simple pet to give a child in a flat. So I made my way down to Van den Goths and saw Mr. Van den Goth himself, a heavily built man who looked like an orangutan carved out of tallow. He placed my terrapins in a cardboard box with moss, and then I asked him if he would mind if I looked round.

A Transport of Terrapins

"Help yourself," he said. "Help yourself." And he lumbered back to his chair and picked up a Dutch newspaper which he was reading, stuck a cigar in his face, and ignored me. I pottered round for some time examining some of the beautiful snakes that he had and became breathless with admiration over a crate full of iguanas, bright green and frilled and dewlapped like a fairy-tale dragon. Presently I glanced at my watch and saw to my alarm that I had overstayed my time by at least half an hour. So, grabbing my box of terrapins, I said a hurried goodbye to Mr. Van den Goth and left to catch the bus.

What I had not noticed, and it was very remiss of me, was that both the terrapins and the moss which Mr. Van den Goth had put in the box were excessively moist. During my wanderings round the shop this moisture had soaked through the bottom of the cardboard box, with the not unnatural result that, when I had climbed up the stairs to the top of the bus and was just about to take my seat, the entire bottom of the box gave way and a cascade of baby terrapins fell on the floor.

It was fortunate for me that there was only one other occupant on the top of the bus, a slender, military-looking man, with a grey moustache and a monocle, wearing a very well-cut tweed suit and a porkpie hat. He had a carnation in his buttonhole and a malacca cane with a silver knob. I scrabbled madly on the floor collecting the terrapins, but baby terrapins can move with extraordinary speed when they want to and I was heavily outnumbered. Suddenly one of them rushed up the central alley of the bus and turned in by the military-looking man's foot. Feeling it clawing at his well-polished shoe, he glanced down. God, I thought, now I'm in for it! He screwed his monocle more firmly into

91

his eye and surveyed the baby terrapin, which was making a laborious effort to climb over the toe of his shoe. "By George!" he said. "A painted terrapin! *Chrysemys picta!* Haven't seen one for years!"

He looked round to see the source from which this little reptile had emanated and saw me crouched, red-faced, on the floor with baby terrapins running madly in all directions.

"Hah!" he said. "Is this little chap yours?"

"Yes, sir," I said. "I'm sorry, but the bottom has fallen out of the box."

"By George, you're in a bit of a stew, what?" he shouted.

"Er . . . yes . . . I am, actually."

He picked up the baby terrapin that had managed to get on the toe of his shoe and came down the bus towards me.

"Here," he said, "let me help. I'll head the bounders off."

"It's very kind of you," I said.

He got down on his hands and knees in the same position that I was in, and we crawled together up and down the bus collecting baby terrapins.

"Tally-ho!" he would shout at intervals. "There's one going under that seat there."

Once, when a small terrapin approached him at a run, he pointed his malacca cane at it and said, "Bang! Bang! Back, sir, or I'll have you on a charge."

Eventually, after about a quarter of an hour of this, we managed to get all the baby terrapins back into the box and I did a rough splinting job on it with my handkerchief.

"It was very kind of you, sir," I said. "I'm afraid you've got your knees all dusty."

"Well worth it," he said. "Well worth it. Haven't had sport like that for a long time."

He screwed his monocle more firmly in his eye and gazed at me.

"Tell me," he said, "what are you doing with a great box full of terrapins?"

"I . . . I work in a pet shop and I've just been down to the wholesalers to get them."

"Oh, I see," he said. "Do you mind if I come and sit near you and have a chin-wag?"

"No, sir," I said. "No."

He came and planted himself firmly on the seat opposite mine, put his malacca cane between his knees, and rested his chin on it and gazed at me thoughtfully.

"Pet shop, eh?" he said. "Hmmm. Do you like animals?"

"Yes, very much. They're about the only thing I do like."

"Hmmm," he said. "What else have you got in this shop?"

He seemed genuinely interested and so I told him about what we had in the shop and about Mr. Romilly, and I was wondering whether to tell him about Mr. Bellow, but I had been sworn to secrecy on that so I decided not to. When we got to my stop I got to my feet.

"I'm sorry, sir," I said. "I've got to get off here."

"Hah," he said. "Hah. Yes, so have I. So have I."

It was perfectly obvious that this was not his stop and that he wanted to continue talking to me. We got down on to the pavement. My rather liberal and eccentric upbringing had left me in no doubt as to the arts and wiles of a pederast. I knew, for example, that even military-looking gentlemen with monocles could be thus inclined, and the fact that he had got off at a stop that was not his argued an interest in me which I felt might possibly turn out to be unsavory. I was cautious.

"Where's your shop, then?" he said, swinging his cane between his finger and thumb.

"Just over there, sir," I said.

"Ah, then I'll walk there with you."

He strolled down the pavement gazing intently at the shops as we passed.

"Tell me," he said, "what do you do with yourself in your spare time?"

"Oh, I go to the zoo and the cinema and to museums and things," I said.

"Do you ever go to the Science Museum?" he inquired. "All those models, and things like that?"

"I like that very much," I said. "I like models."

"Do you? Do you?" he said, screwing his monocle in and glaring at me. "You like to play, do you?"

"Well, I suppose you could call it that," I said.

"Ah," he said.

We paused outside the door of the Aquarium.

"Well, if you'll excuse me, sir," I said, "I'm . . . I'm rather late as it is."

"Wondered," he said. "Wondered."

He pulled out a wallet and extracted from it a card.

"There's my name and address. If you'd like to come round one evening, we could play a game."

"That's, er . . . very kind of you, sir," I said, keeping my back firmly to the wall.

"Don't mention it," he said. "Hope to see you, then. Don't bother to ring up . . . just call. I'm always there. Any time after six."

He strolled off down the street, very much the military man. There was no trace of mincing or of effeminacy about him, but I was not so innocent as not to know that these were not essential manifestations of homosexuality in a person's character. I stuffed his card into my pocket and went into the shop.

"Where have you *been*, you naughty boy?" asked Mr. Romilly.

"I'm sorry I'm late," I said. "But . . . but I . . . I had a little accident on the bus. The bottom fell out of the box and all the terrapins got out, and a colonel chappy helped me to pick them all up but it delayed us a bit. I'm very sorry, Mr. Romilly.'

"That's all right, that's all right," he said. "It's been a very quiet afternoon. Very quiet . . . very quiet. Now, I've got the tank ready for them if you'd like to put them in."

So I put the baby terrapins in the tank and watched them swimming about, and then I took out the Colonel's card and looked at it. "Colonel Anstruther" it said, "47 Bell Mews, South Kensington," and then it had a telephone number. I mused on it for a bit.

"Mr. Romilly," I said, "you don't know a Colonel Anstruther, do you?"

"Anstruther? Anstruther?" said Mr. Romilly, frowning. "I can't say that I do. . . . Ah, but wait a bit, wait a bit. Where does he live?"

"Bell Mews," I said.

"That's him. That's him!" said Mr. Romilly, delighted. "Yes, yes . . . yes. That's him. A fine soldier. And a very fine man, too. Was he the person that helped you pick up the terrapins?"

"Yes," I said.

"Ah, just like him. Always a man to help a friend in need," said Mr. Romilly. "They don't breed them like that nowadays, you know. They don't breed them like that at all."

95

"So he's . . . um . . . well known and, er . . . respected?" I said.

"Oh, yes, indeed. Yes, indeed. Everyone knows him in that area. They're all very fond of the old Colonel."

I pondered on this information for some time, and then I thought that perhaps I would take the Colonel up on his invitation. After all, I thought, if worst came to worst I could always scream for help. In spite of the fact that he told me not to ring, I thought I had better be polite, so a few days later I phoned him up.

"Colonel Anstruther?" I asked.

"Yes. Yes," he said. "Who's that? Who's that?"

"It's, um . . . my name is . . . Durrell," I said. "I met you on the bus the other evening. You were kind enough to help me catch up my terrapins."

"Oh, yes," he said. "Yes. How are the little chaps?"

"Fine," I said. "They're . . . they're doing fine. I wondered if, perhaps, I could . . . take you up on your kind offer of coming round to see you?"

"But of course, my dear chap. Of course!" he said. "Delighted! Delighted! What time will you be here?"

"Well, what time would be convenient?" I asked.

"Come round about six thirty," he said; "come to dinner."

"Thank you very much," I said. "I'll be there."

Bell Mews, I discovered, was a short, cobbled cul-de-sac with four small houses on each side. But I was confused at first because every door on one side was labelled "47." What I did not know was that the Colonel owned all four houses and had knocked them into one and, with a brilliant display of the military mind, had labelled each door with the same number. So after some moments of hesitation I finally knocked on the nearest door marked "47" and waited to see what would happen. While I waited I reflected upon the stupidity of having four houses in a mews a couple of hundred yards long all labelled "47," and if it came to that, where were all the other numbers? They were presumably scattered round the various roads and mews in the vicinity. The postman's lot in London, I felt, must be a very unhappy one.

At that moment, the door that I had knocked on was flung open and there stood the Colonel. He was dressed, to my consternation, in a bottle-green velvet smoking jacket with watered silk lapels, and he brandished in one hand a carving knife of prodigious dimensions. I began to wonder whether I had been wise to come after all.

"Durrell?" he said, screwing his monocle into his eye. "By Jove, you're punctual!"

"Well, I had a little difficulty," I began.

"Ah!" he said. "The forty-seven foxed you, did it? It foxes them all. Gives me a bit of privacy, you know. Come in! Come in!"

I edged my way into the hall and he closed the door. "Good to see you," he said. "Come along."

He led the way, at a brisk trot, through the hall, holding the carving knife out in front of him as though leading a cavalry charge. I had a brief glimpse of a mahogany hat-stand and some prints on the wall, and then we were in a large, spacious living room, simply but comfortably furnished, with piles of books everywhere and color reproductions of various military uniforms on the walls. He led me through this and into the large kitchen.

"Sorry to rush you," he panted. "But I've got a pie in the oven and I don't want to get it burnt."

He rushed over to the oven and opened it and peered inside.

"Ah, no, that's all right," he said. "Good . . . good."
He straightened up and looked at me.

"Do you like steak and kidney pie?" he inquired.

"Er, yes," I said. "I'm very fond of it."

"Good," he said. "It'll be ready in a moment or two.
Now, come and sit down and have a drink,"
He led me back into the living room.

"Sit you down, sit you down," he said. "What'll you
drink? Sherry? Whisky? Gin?"

"You, er . . . haven't got any wine, have you?" I said.

"Wine?" he said. "Yes, of course, of course."

He got out a bottle, uncorked it, and poured me a
glass full of ruby-red wine which was crisp and dry. We
sat chatting (mainly about terrapins) for ten minutes or
so and then the Colonel glanced at his watch.

"Should be ready now," he said, "should be ready.
You don't mind eating in the kitchen, do you? It saves
a lot of mucking about."

"No, I don't mind at all," I said.

We went into the kitchen and the Colonel laid the
table and then he mashed some potatoes and heaped a
great mound of steak and kidney pudding onto them and
put the plate in front of me.

"Have some more wine," he said.

The steak and kidney was excellent. I inquired
whether the Colonel had made it himself.

"Yes," he said. "Had to learn to cook when my wife
died. Quite simple, really, if you put your mind to it. It's
a wonder what you can do with a pinch of herbs here
and there, and that sort of thing, you know. Do you
cook?"

"Well, in a rather vague sort of way," I said. "My
mother has taught me a few things, but I've never done
it very seriously. I like it."

98

"So do I," he said. "So do I. Relaxes the mind."

After we had finished off the steak and kidney pudding he got some ice cream out of the fridge and we ate that.

"Ah," said the Colonel, leaning back in his chair and patting his stomach, "that's better. That's better. I only have one meal a day and I like to make it a solid one. Now, how about a glass of port? I've got some rather good stuff here."

We had a couple of glasses of port and the Colonel lit up a fine thin cheroot. When we had finished the port and he had stubbed his cheroot out, he screwed his monocle more firmly in his eye and looked at me.

"What about going upstairs for a little game?" he asked.

"Um . . . what sort of game?" I inquired cautiously, feeling that this was the moment when, if he was going to, he would start making advances.

"Power game," said the Colonel. "Battle of wits. Models. You like that sort of thing, don't you?"

"Um . . . yes," I said.

"Come on, then," he said. "Come on."

He led me out into the hall again and then up a staircase, through a small room which was obviously a sort of workshop; there was a bench along one side with shelves upon which were pots of paint, soldering irons, and other mysterious things. Obviously the Colonel was a do-it-yourselfer in his spare time, I thought. Then he threw open a door and a most amazing sight met my gaze. The room I looked into ran the whole width of the house and was some seventy to eighty feet long. It was, in fact, all the top rooms knocked into one of the four mews houses that the Colonel owned. He had turned it all into one gigantic room and the floor was neatly parqueted. But it was not so much the size of the room that astonished me but what it contained. At each end of the room was a large fort made out of papier mâché. They must have been three or four feet high and four or five feet across. Ranged round them were hundreds upon hundreds of tin soldiers, glittering and gleaming in their bright uniforms, and amongst them were tanks, armored trucks, anti-aircraft guns, and similar things. There, spread out before me, was the full panoply of war.

"Ah," said the Colonel, rubbing his hands in glee, "surprised you!"

"Good Lord, yes!" I said. "I don't think I've ever seen so many toy soldiers."

"It's taken me years to amass them," he said. "Years. I get 'em from a factory, you know. I get 'em unpainted and paint 'em myself. Much better that way. Get a smoother, cleaner job. . . . More realistic, too."

I bent down and picked up one of the tiny soldiers. It was quite true, what the Colonel had said. Normally a tin soldier is a fairly botchy job of painting, but these were meticulously done. Even the faces appeared to have expression on them.

"Now," said the Colonel. "Now. We'll have a quick game – just a sort of run-through. Once you get the hang of it we can make it more complicated, of course. Now, I'll explain the rules to you."

The rules of the game, as explained by the Colonel, were fairly straightforward. You each had an army. You threw two dice and the one who got the highest score was the aggressor and it was his turn to start first. He threw his dice and from the number that came up he could move a battalion of his men in any direction that he pleased, and he was allowed to fire off a barrage from his field guns or anti-aircraft guns. These worked on a spring mechanism and you loaded them with matchsticks. The springs in these guns were surprisingly strong and projected the matchsticks with incredible velocity down the room. Wherever a matchstick landed, everything in a radius of some four inches around it was taken to be destroyed. So if you could gain a direct hit on a column of troops you could do savage damage to the enemy. Each player had a little spring tape measure in his pocket for measuring the distance round the matchstick.

I was enchanted by the whole idea, but principally because it reminded me very much of a game that we had invented when we were in Greece. My brother Leslie, whose interest in guns and boats is insatiable, had collected a whole navy of toy battleships, cruisers, and submarines, and we would range these out on the floor and play a game very similar to the Colonel's game, only we used marbles in order to score direct hits on the ships. Rolling a marble accurately over a bumpy floor in order to hit a destroyer an inch and a half long took a keen eye.

It turned out, after we had thrown the first dice, that I was to be the aggressor.

"Hah!" said the Colonel. "Filthy Hun!"

I could see that he was working himself into a warlike mood.

"Is the object of the exercise to try and capture your fort?" I inquired.

"Well, you can do that," he said. "Or you can knock it out, *if* you can.

I soon discovered that the way to play the Colonel's game was to distract his attention from one flank so that you could do some quick maneuvering while he was unaware of it, so I kept up a constant barrage on his troops, the matches whistling down the room, and while doing this I moved a couple of battalions up close to his lines.

"Swine!" the Colonel would roar every time a matchstick fell and he had to measure the distance. "Dirty swine! Bloody Hun!" His face grew quite pink and his eyes watered copiously so that he had to keep removing his monocle and polishing it.

"You're too bloody accurate," he shouted.

"Well, it's your fault," I shouted back. "You're keeping all your troops bunched together. They make an ideal target."

"It's part of me strategy. Don't question me strategy. I'm *older* than you, *and* superior in rank."

"How can you be superior in rank, when I'm in command of an army?"

"No lip out of you, you whippersnapper," he roared.

So the game went on for about two hours, by which time I had successfully knocked out most of the Colonel's troops and got a foothold at the bottom of his fort.

"Do you surrender?" I shouted.

"Never!" said the Colonel. "Never! Surrender to a bloody Hun? Never!"

"Well, in that case I'm going to bring my sappers in," I said.

"What are you going to do with your sappers?"

"Blow up your fort," I said.

"You can't do that," he said. "Against the articles of war."

"Nonsense!" I said. "The Germans don't care about articles of war, anyway."

"That's a filthy trick to play!" he roared, as I successfully detonated his fort.

"Now do you surrender?"

"No. I'll fight you every inch of the way, you Hun!" he shouted, crawling rapidly across the floor on his hands and knees and frantically moving his troops. But all his efforts were of no avail: I had him pinned in a corner and I shot him to pieces.

"By George!" said the Colonel when it was all over, mopping his brow, "I've never seen anybody play the game like that. How did you manage to get so damned accurate when you haven't played it before?"

"Well, I've played a similar game, only we used marbles," I said. "But I think once you've got your eye in it, it helps."

"Gad!" said the Colonel, looking at the destruction of his army. "Still, it was a good game and a good fight. Shall we have another one?"

So we played on and on, the Colonel getting more and more excited, until at last I glanced at my watch and saw to my horror that it was one o'clock in the morning. We were in the middle of a game and so we left the troops where they were and on the following night I went back and finished it. After that I would spend two or three evenings a week with the Colonel, fighting battles up and down the long room, and it gave him tremendous pleasure – almost as much pleasure as it gave me.

Not long after that, Mother announced that she had finally found a house and that we could move out of London. I was bitterly disappointed. It meant that I would have to give up my job and lose contact with my friends Mr. Bellow and Colonel Anstruther. Mr. Romilly was heart-broken.

"I shall never find anybody to replace you," he said. "Never."

"Oh, there'll be somebody along," I said.

"Ah, but not with your ability to decorate cages and things," said Mr. Romilly. "I don't know what I'm going to do without you."

When the day finally came for me to leave, with tears in his eyes he presented me with a leather wallet. On the inside it had embossed in gold, "To Gerald Durrell from his fellow workers." I was a bit puzzled since there had been only Mr. Romilly and myself, but I suppose that he thought it looked better like that. I thanked him very much and then I made my way for the last time down Potts Lane to Mr. Bellow's establishment.

"Sorry to see you go, boy," he said. "Very sorry indeed. Here . . . I've got this for you – a little parting present."

He put a small square cage in my hands and sitting inside it was the bird that I most coveted in his collection, the red cardinal. I was overwhelmed.

"Are you sure you want me to have it?" I asked.

"Course I am, boy. Course I am."

"But, is it the right time of year for giving a present like this?" I inquired.

Mr. Bellow guffawed.

"Yes, of course it is," he said. "Of course it is."

I took my leave of him and then I went round that evening to play a last game with the Colonel. When it was over – I had let him win – he led me downstairs.

"Shall miss you, you know, my boy. Shall miss you greatly. However, keep in touch, won't you? Keep in touch. I've got a little, um . . . a little souvenir here for you."

He handed me a slim silver cigarette case. On it had been written, "With love from Margery." I was a bit puzzled by this.

"Oh, take no notice of the inscription," he said. "You can have it removed . . . Present from a woman . . . I knew once. Thought you'd like it. Memento, hmmm?"

"It's very, very kind of you, sir," I said.

"Not at all, not at all," he said, and blew his nose and polished his monocle and held out his hand. "Well, good luck, my boy. And I hope I'll see you again one day."

I never did see him again. He died several months later.

❊ A Question of Promotion ❊

MAMFE IS NOT the most salubrious of places, perched
as it is on a promontory above the curve of a great,
brown river and surrounded by dense rain forest. It is
as hot and moist as a Turkish bath for most of the year,
only deviating from this monotony during the rainy
season, when it becomes hotter and moister.

At that time it had a resident population of five
white men, one white woman, and some ten thousand
vociferous Africans. In a moment of mental aberration
I had made this my headquarters for an animal collection expedition and was occupying a large marquee full
of assorted wild animals on the banks of the brown,
hippo-reverberating river. In the course of my work I
had, of course, come to know the white population
fairly well and a vast number of the African population.
Africans acted as my hunters, guides, and carriers, for
when you went into that forest you were transported
back into the days of Stanley and Livingstone and all
your worldly possessions had to be carried on the heads
of a line of stalwart carriers.

Collecting wild animals is a full-time occupation
and one does not have much time for the social graces,
and so it was curious that in this unlikely spot I had the
opportunity of helping what was then known as the
Colonial Office.

A Question of Promotion

I was busy one morning with the task of giving milk to five unweaned baby squirrels, none of whom, it appeared, had any brain or any desire to live. At that time no feeding bottle with a teat small enough to fit the minute mouth of a baby squirrel had been invented, so the process was to wrap cotton wool round the end of a matchstick, dip it in the milk mixture, and put it into their mouths for them to suck. This was a prolonged and extremely irritating job, for you had to be careful not to put too much milk on the cotton wool, otherwise they would choke, and you had to slip the cotton wool into their mouths sideways, otherwise it would catch on their teeth, whereupon they would promptly swallow it and die of an impacted bowel.

It was ten o'clock in the morning and already the heat was so intense that I had to keep wiping my hands on a towel so that I would not drench the baby squirrels with my sweat and thus give them a chill. I was not in the best of tempers but while I was trying to get some sustenance into my protégés (who were not co-operating), my steward, Pious, suddenly materialized at my side in his usual silent, unnerving way.

"Please, sah," he said.

"Yes, whatee?" I inquired irritably, trying to push some milk-drenched cotton wool into a squirrel's mouth.

"D.O. come, sah," he said.

"The District Officer?" I asked in astonishment. "What the hell does he want?"

"No say, sah," said Pious impassively. "I go open beer?"

"Well, I suppose you'd better," I said, and as Martin Bugler, the District Officer, arrived at the crest of the hill above my camp I pushed the squirrels back into their nestbox full of dried banana leaves and went out of the marquee to greet him.

Martin was a tall, gangling young man with round, almost-black eyes and floppy black hair, a snub nose, and a wide, ingratiating grin. Owing to the length of his arms and legs and his habit of making wild gestures to illustrate when he talked, he was accident prone. But he was, however, a remarkably good D.O., for he loved his job intensely and, what is even more important, he loved the Africans equally as much and they responded to this.

Now it has become fashionable to run down colonialism, District Officers and their assistants are made out to be monsters of iniquity. Of course there were bad ones but the majority of them were a wonderful set of men who did an exceedingly difficult job under the most trying conditions. Imagine, at the age of twenty-eight being put in charge of an area, say, the size of Wales, populated by an enormous number of Africans and with one assistant to help you. You had to look after their every need, you had to be mother and father to them, and you had to dispense the law. And in many cases the law, being English law, was of such complexity that it defeated even the devious brain of the indigenous population.

On many occasions on my forays into the forest I had passed the big mud-brick courtroom with its tin roof and seen Martin – the sweat pouring down him in torrents – trying some case or other, the whole thing being made even more complicated by the fact that villages, sometimes separated only by a few miles, spoke a different dialect. Therefore, should there be dissension between two villages, it meant that you had to have an interpreter from each of the two villages and an interpreter who knew both dialects who could then interpret Martin. As in courts of law anywhere in the world, you knew perfectly well that everybody was lying the hind leg off a donkey, and I had the greatest admiration for Martin's patience and solemnity on these occasions. The cases could range from suspected cannibalism, through wife-stealing, to simple things like whose cocoa-yam patch was invading whose, inch by subtle inch.

On the many occasions when I visited West Africa, I met only one D.O. who was unpleasant. By and large, as I say, they were a wonderful bunch of young men and somebody someday ought to write a book in their praise.

I was very surprised at Martin's appearance because at that time in the morning he should have been up to his eyes in office work. He came down the hillside almost at a run, gesticulating like a windmill and shouting things at me that I could not hear. I waited patiently until he reached the shade of the marquee.

"So you see," he said, throwing out his arms in a gesture of despair, "I need help."

I pushed a camp chair forward and pressed him gently into it.

"Now stop carrying on like a mentally defective praying mantis," I said. "Just shut up for a minute and relax."

He sat there mopping his brow with a sodden handkerchief.

"Pious!" I shouted.

"Sah," replied Pious from the kitchen.

"Pass beer for me and the D.O. please."

"Yes, sah."

The beer was of a nauseating brand and not really cold because in our rather primitive base camp the only method of refrigeration was to keep the beer in buckets of water, and the water was always lukewarm. However, in climates like that, where you perspire constantly – even when sitting immobile – you need a large liquid intake and for the daytime beer was the best.

Pious gravely poured the beer out into the glasses

and Martin picked his up with a shaking hand and took a couple of frenzied gulps.

"Now," I said, putting on my best soothing-psychiatrist voice, "do you mind repeating, slowly and clearly, what you were shouting as you came down the hill? And, by the way, you shouldn't run about like that at this hour of the day. A, it's bad for your health and, B, it doesn't do your public image any good. I thought you'd had a terrible uprising in Mamfe and that you were being pursued by vast quantities of Africans with spears and muzzle-loaders."

Martin mopped his face and took another gulp of beer.

"It's *worse* than that," he said, "much, *much* worse."

"Well," I said, "softly and calmly tell me what's the matter."

"It's the District Commissioner," he said.

"What's the matter with him?" I inquired. "Has he sacked you?"

"That's the point," said Martin. "He well might. That's why I want help."

"I don't see how *I* can help," I said. "I don't know the District Commissioner or, as far as I am aware, any of his relatives, so I can't put in a good word for you. Why, what heinous crime have you committed?"

"I suppose I had better begin at the beginning," said Martin.

He mopped his face again, took another sustaining gulp of beer and glanced round furtively to make sure that we weren't overheard.

"Well," he said, "you probably haven't noticed, but I'm quite good at my *job*, but unfortunately when it comes to entertaining and things like that I always seem to manage to do the wrong things. When I had just been promoted to D.O. – that was in Umfala – the first thing that happened was that the bloody D.C. came through on a tour of inspection. Everything went splendidly. I had my district in apple-pie order and it seemed as though the D.C. was rather pleased with me. He was only staying one night and by evening I really thought that the whole thing had been a success. But it was very unfortunate that the lavatory in my house had ceased to function and I couldn't get it fixed in time so I had had a very comfortable grass shack built well away from the veranda, behind the hibiscus hedge. You know, a hole in the ground and a cross-pole on which you sit. Well, I explained this to the D.C. and it seemed that he quite understood. What I hadn't realized was that my entire African staff supposed that I had built it for them and had been using it for several days before the D.C.'s arrival. Just before dinner the D.C. wandered out to the latrine. The first problem was that the contents rather put him off, since he was under the impression that the latrine had been built specially for him. And then he sat on the cross-pole, which broke."

It was my turn now to become slightly alarmed.

"God in heaven," I said, "didn't you check the cross-pole?"

"That's the point," said Martin. "I am so *bad* at that sort of thing."

"But you might have killed him or, worse still, drowned him," I said. "I know what our latrine's like here and I certainly wouldn't like to fall into it."

"I can assure you he didn't enjoy the experience either," said Martin dismally. "He shouted for help of course and we got him out, but he looked like a sort of, er . . . a sort of, er . . . sort of walking dung heap. It took us hours to wash him down and get his clothes washed and cleaned in time for his departure the following morning, and I can assure you, my dear boy, we sat down to a very late dinner and he ate very little and the conversation was frigid to an almost polar degree."

"Hasn't he any spirit of fun?" I inquired.

"He hasn't any spirit of fun about anything," said Martin vehemently. "And anyway, I don't blame him. Anyone falling into that load of muck couldn't possibly treat it with merriment."

"I do see your point," I said. "Have some more beer."

"The trouble is," said Martin, "that this was not the first time that I'd made mistakes of this sort. There are several things I did when I was an A.D.O. which I prefer not to tell you about, and that's why it took me so long to work up from being an A.D.O. to a D.O. After this awful lavatory thing my next posting was to Umchichi, and you know what *that's* like."

"Dear God," I said, "I've never been there but I've heard about it."

Umchichi was the sort of Devil's Island to which all naughty D.O.'s and A.D.O.'s were sent when they were in disgrace. It consisted of a lot of leprous Africans and more mosquitoes than anywhere else on the whole west coast of Africa.

"Fascinating though these revelations are," I said, "I don't really see what this is all about."

"But that's what I was *telling* you as I was coming down the hill," explained Martin. "He's coming through on a tour of inspection. He arrives in three days' time so I *must* have your help."

"Martin," I said, "much as I love you, I am not a social hostess."

"No, no, old boy, I know," he said, "but if you could just back me up a bit."

A Question of Promotion

This *cri de cœur* was impossible to refuse. All the white population of Mamfe and ninety-nine per cent of the African population loved Martin dearly.

"I must give this some thought," I said.

We sat in silence while Martin twitched and perspired. Presently I shouted, "Pious, pass more beer for the D.O. please."

When the beer had been served I leaned forward and fixed Martin with a piercing eye.

"This," I said, "is your only salvation. We have a woman in our midst."

"A woman?" said Martin, puzzled. "What woman?"

"Mary," I said, "your A.D.O.'s wife, in case you hadn't remembered. Now women are good at this sort of thing. We also have McGrade [he was the Public Works Department man in charge of mending bridges, building roads, and other mundane things]. We have Girton [he was the United Africa Company man, who spent his time selling Manchester cloth to the Africans and beer and tinned goods to the white population]. Now, surely between all of us we can get something done."

"Dear boy," said Martin solemnly, "I shall be forever in your debt. What a brilliant suggestion."

"Now, the first thing to do," I said, "is to have a look at your house."

"But you've been there often," said Martin in surprise. "You've been up several times for chop and any number of times for drinks."

"Yes," I said, "but I've never seen anything other than your main living room and your veranda."

"Oh, I see what you mean," he said. "Yes, of course. Well, you'd better come up and see it now."

"I'll bring Pious," I said, "because I'll lend you him for the evening. He's far better than that stupid lout you've got and he can really put on Government House type service. That steward of yours is liable to drop the soup in the D.C.'s lap."

"Oh, God!" said Martin in an agonized tone of voice, "don't even suggest such a thing."

So, taking Pious with us, we went up to the D.O.'s house, which was perched high on a bluff overlooking the river. It was a very handsome house, with thick walls and huge rooms, for it had been built in the time when the Cameroons had been a German colony, and the Germans knew how to build for the heat so the house received what little breeze there was, and the massive walls made its interior as cool as possible in a place like Mamfe. On the way up the hill I explained to Pious what the problem was.

"Now," I said, "this is very important and we all go help the D.O. as well as we can."

"Yes, sah," said Pious grinning happily, for he always felt I spent far too much time looking after my animals and not nearly enough time letting him show off his prowess as a steward.

When we got there I examined the living room and the veranda with great attention. They were spacious and quite pleasantly furnished by bachelor D.O. standards.

"I think you ought to take that calendar off the wall for a start," I said to Martin.

"Why?" he asked. "I thought she was awfully pretty."

"Martin," I said, "if the D.C. sees nude women hanging all over your living room, he is going to get some very peculiar ideas about you, so take it down."

Pious, who had been following this with close attention, took down the calendar of a woman in a voluptuous pose who was so obviously a mammal that it almost embarrassed *me.*

"Now, his bedroom," I said.

The bedroom, again, was large and contained a big double bed with a mosquito net.

"Pious," I said, "you go look the bed to make sure it no go break."

Giggling happily to himself, Pious crawled round the bed on hands and knees examining every nut and bolt.

"Now," I said to Martin, "we'll both bounce up and down on top of it."

We did and the bed responded well.

"Well, that's all right," I said. "I don't think there's anything in here that will do him any damage. Now, where are you going to feed him?"

"Feed him?" said Martin, puzzled.

"You *are* going to feed him while he's here, aren't you?" I said impatiently.

"Well, on the veranda," Martin said.

"But haven't you got anything else?" I asked.

"There's the dining room."

"If you've got a dining room, for God's sake use it. After all, you want to give him the best treatment possible. Where *is* this dining room?"

He took me to the living room, threw open two massive wooden doors, and there was a splendid dining room with a table long enough to seat at least ten people. It was beautifully polished but, naturally, as Martin had never used the room, the table was covered in dust, as were the rather handsome but heavy wooden chairs. From the ceiling, down the whole length of this fifteen-foot table hung what in India is called a "punkah." It is, in fact, a giant fan. The backbone of this one was made of a long length of bamboo four or five inches in diameter, and from it hung down a fringe of dried palm fronds some four feet in length. From the centre of the bamboo ran a string through a series of little pulleys across the ceiling and out through a hole in the wall which led to the kitchen quarters. The idea was that you engaged a small boy to pull the string so that the fan waved to and fro over the table, thus occasionally allowing you a gust of warm air in the midst of your meal.

"But this is absolutely splendid," I said to Martin. "He'll be most impressed."

"I never use the damn thing," said Martin. "You see, I would feel so lonely sitting here."

"What you want is a wife, my boy," I said in a fatherly tone.

"Well, I do try," said Martin, "every time I go on leave. But as soon as they hear where I am, they break off the engagement."

"Never mind," I said. "Persevere. You might find a woman stupid enough to marry you in the first place and live here one day."

We got Pious to examine the huge table and the chairs with great care. We both sat on each one of them and tested the table by standing on it and doing a sort of tango, but it was as firm and solid as rock.

"Now," I said to Martin, "I want to put Pious in charge of your staff because by and large they seem a very inefficient lot. Pious is highly efficient."

"Anything you say, dear boy, anything at all," said Martin. "Just mention it."

"Pious," I said, "we have three days to get ready. During that time you go be half my steward and half the D.O.'s steward. You hear?"

"I hear, sah," he said.

We went out onto the veranda and sat down.

"Now," I said to Pious, "go tell the D.O.'s steward to pass us a drink. By the way, Martin, what is the name of your steward?" I asked.

"Amos," he replied.

I said, "Well, Pious, go tell Amos to pass drink and then you go bring the cook, the steward, and the small boy here so we look 'um and have palava."

"Yes, sah," said Pious, and with an almost military strut he disappeared in the direction of the kitchen.

"I think the question of the food can be safely left to Mary," I said. "The others might have some suggestions of use, too, so what I think would be a good thing is to call a council of war this evening. If you send chits round to all of them they can come up and have drinks and we can discuss the whole matter."

"You're really proving my salvation," said Martin.

"Nonsense," I said. "I am just orientating you a bit. You obviously aren't cut out for social life."

Pious came in bearing a tray with beer, followed by Amos, in brown shorts and jacket; the small boy, who looked quite bright but was obviously completely untrained and – if Amos was supposed to be his trainer – never would learn a thing; and then, to my astonishment, an enormous, tall, thin Hausa who looked as though he was a hundred and ten years old, wearing a white coat and shorts and a huge chef's hat, on the front of which was embroidered in rather uneven lettering "B.C."

"Now," I said in my firmest voice, "the D.O. is having the D.C. here in three days' time. The D.O. he want my steward to watch you all and make sure that everything is proper. If it is not proper, D.C. will be very angry with D.O., and D.O. and I will be very angry with you and we will kick you for larse."

In spite of the sternness with which I spoke, they all grinned at me happily. They knew the importance of the visitor and they knew that my threat was quite genuine. But it was put in a joking form that they could understand.

"Now," I said, pointing to Martin's steward, "you're named Amos."

"Yes, sah," he said, standing to attention.

"Now, whatee your name?" I asked the small boy.

"John, sah," he said.

"The cook," said Martin apologetically, interrupting my dragooning, "is called Jesus."

"Dear fellow," I said, "you're in luck. With Pious and Jesus with us we can't go far wrong. By the way, what is that extraordinary piece of embroidery on the front of his hat?"

Martin looked acutely embarrassed.

"He happened to cook a very good meal one day by pure accident," said Martin, "and I had a magazine which had a picture of a chef in a London hotel and so to encourage him I told him that the next time I went on leave I would buy him one of these hats that only expert cooks wore."

"It was a very kind thought," I said, "but what's the embroidery in the front, the 'B.C.'?"

Martin looked very shamefaced.

"He got his wife to embroider that on for him," he said, "and he's very proud of it."

"But what does it mean?" I insisted.

Martin looked even more embarrassed.

"It means Bugler's cook," he said.

"Does he realize the terrible confusion he could cause in some people's mind by being called Jesus and having 'B.C.' on his hat?" I inquired.

"No, I've never tried to explain it to him," said Martin. "I felt it would only worry him and he's quite worried enough as it is."

I took a long soothing draught of beer. The whole thing appeared to be getting so religious one would have thought it was the Pope who was arriving instead of the D.C.

"Now, Pious," I said, "you go get some furniture oil, you hear?"

"Yes, sah," he said.

"And," I said, "you go make sure that the dining room is cleaned out and the chairs and table are polished proper. You hear?"

"I hear, sah," he said.

"I want the table top to look like a mirror. And if you don't make sure that it does, I'll kick your larse."

"Yes, sah," he said.

"And then the day before the D.C. arrive, all the floors have to be scrubbed and made clean and all the other furniture polished too. You hear?"

"Yes, sah," said Pious.

I could see by the proud look on his face that he was going to look forward immensely to overseeing this very important occasion and also having the opportunity of dominating some of his compatriots.

Martin leant forward and whispered in my ear. "The small boy is an Ibo," he said.

Now, the Ibos are an extremely clever tribe and were constantly wandering over from Nigeria, swindling the

Cameroonians and wandering back again. So they were regarded by the Cameroonians with great loathing and distrust.

"Pious," I said, "the small boy is Ibo."

"I know, sah," said Pious.

"So you go make him work hard but you no go make him work too hard because he is an Ibo. You hear?"

"Yes, sah," said Pious.

"All right," I said as though I owned Martin's house, "pass more beer."

The staff trooped off into the kitchen.

"I say," said Martin in admiration, "you are good at this sort of thing, aren't you?"

"I've never done it before," I said, "but it doesn't require much imagination."

"No, I'm afraid I'm rather lacking in that," said Martin.

"I don't think you are lacking in imagination," I said. "Anybody who would have the brilliance to bring back a chef's hat for his cook cannot be completely insensitive."

So we drank some more beer and I tried to think of any other calamity that could possibly happen.

"Does the lavatory work?" I asked suspiciously.

"It's working perfectly."

"Well, don't, for God's sake, let the small boy drop a pawpaw down it," I said, "because we don't want a repetition of the last episode you told me about. Now, you send the chits round to everybody and I'll come up here about six o'clock and we'll have a conference of war."

"Wonderful," said Martin. He put his hand on my shoulder and squeezed it affectionately. "I don't know what I'd do without you," he said. "Even Standish couldn't have organized things so beautifully."

Standish was the Assistant D.O. and was at that

moment sweating his way through the mountains north of Mamfe, sorting out the problems of the remoter villages.

I hurried back to my marquee and my vociferous family. Helping Martin had set me back in my routine work so the baby chimps were yelling for their food, porcupines were champing at the bars, and the bush-babies with enormous eyes glared at me indignantly because they had found no pots of delicately chopped fruit in their cages.

At six o'clock I presented myself at the D.O.'s residence and found that Mary Standish had already arrived. She was a young and pretty woman, inclined to plumpness, and had a great placidity of nature. She had been whisked by Standish from some obscure place like Surbiton or Penge and had been plonked down in the middle of Mamfe. She had been there only six months but she was so gentle and sweet and accepted everything and everybody with such calmness and good nature that you felt that if you had a raging headache and she placed one of her plump little hands on your forehead, it would have the same effect as an eau de cologne-soaked handkerchief.

"Gerry," she squeaked, "isn't this exciting?"

"Well, it may be for you," I said, "but it's a pain in the neck as far as poor Martin is concerned."

"But the D.C.!" she said. "It might mean a promotion for Martin and it might even mean one for Alec."

"If it's organized properly," I said. "The reason we're having this council of war is to make sure that nothing goes wrong because, as you know, Martin is accident prone. . . ."

Martin, thinking that I was going to tell her the hideous story of the D.C. and the latrine, made one of his windmill gestures to stop me and immediately knocked his glass of beer onto the floor.

"Sorry, sah," said Amos. The Cameroonians had an endearing habit of saying "Sorry, sah" whenever any accident befell you, as though it were their own fault. If, for example, you were leading a line of carriers in the forest and you tripped over a root and grazed your knee, you would hear "Sorry, sah," "Sorry, sah," "Sorry, sah," "Sorry, sah," echoing back along the whole line of carriers.

"You see what I mean?" I said to Mary as Amos cleaned up the mess and brought Martin a fresh glass of beer.

"Yes, I do see," she said.

Waiting for the others to arrive, we drank our beer thoughtfully and listened to the hippos gurgling and roaring and snorting in the river some three hundred feet below us.

Presently McGrade arrived. He was a very impressive Irishman of enormous dimensions with almost pillar-box-red hair and vivid blue eyes, and he had one of those lovely Irish accents that are as soft as cream being poured out of a jug. He slumped his massive form onto a chair, seized Martin's glass of beer, drank deeply from it, and said, "So you're being visited by royalty, then?"

"The nearest approach to it," said Martin, "and kindly give me back my beer. I'm in urgent need of it."

"Is he coming by road?" inquired McGrade anxiously.

"I think so," said Martin. "Why?"

"Well, I wouldn't give that old bridge very much longer," said McGrade. "I think if he came across that we might well have to bury him here."

The bridge he was referring to was an iron suspension bridge that spanned the river at one point and had been built in the early 1900s. I had crossed it many times myself and knew that it was highly unsafe, but it was my one means of getting into the forest so I always had my carriers go across one at a time. As a matter of fact, McGrade's prediction about the bridge was perfectly correct, because not many months later a whole load of tribesmen came down from the mountain regions carrying sacks of rice on their heads and all crossed the bridge simultaneously, whereupon it collapsed and they crashed a hundred feet or so into the gorge below. But Africans, by and large, are rather like Greeks. They take these unusual incidents in their stride and so not one of the Africans was hurt, and the thing that annoyed them most was that they lost their rice.

"But he can't come across the bridge, can he?" said Martin, anxiously looking round at our faces. "Not unless he's coming with carriers."

McGrade leaned forward and patted Martin solemnly on the head. "I was only joking," he said. "All the roads and bridges that he will have to cross to get here are in perfect condition. When you want a job well done you get an Irishman."

"Now," I said, "we've got a Catholic in our midst as well as a Pious and a Jesus."

"You," said McGrade, smiling at me affectionately and rumpling his mop of crimson hair, "are just a bloody heathen animal collector."

"And you," I said, "spend more time in the bloody confessional than mending the atrocious roads and bridges around here."

At that moment Robin Girton arrived. He was a small, dark man with a hawk-like nose and large brown eyes that always had a dreamy expression and gave you the impression that he wasn't really with you. But he was, in fact, like all the United Africa Company people I had come across, exceedingly astute. He never spoke unless it was absolutely necessary and generally sat there looking as though he was in a trance. Then, suddenly, in a soft voice that had a faint tinge of North Country in it, he would come out with a remark so pertinent and intelligent that it summed up succinctly what everybody else had been arguing about for an hour and a half. The effect was positively startling.

He arranged himself elegantly in a chair, accepted a glass of beer, and then glanced round at our faces.

"Isn't it exciting?" said Mary with great enthusiasm.

Robin sipped his beer and nodded his head gravely.

"I gather," he said, "that we have been summoned here to do Martin's work for him as usual."

"Now, hold on," said Mary indignantly.

"If you've come here in that sort of a mood, I'd rather you left," said Martin.

"We'll leave when your beer runs out," said McGrade.

"What do you mean," said Martin, "doing my work for me?"

"Well," said Robin, "I do far more good for the community by selling them baked beans and yard upon yard of Manchester-manufactured cloth carefully embossed with aeroplanes than you do running around hanging them right, left, and centre for murdering their grandmothers, who probably deserved to die in the first place."

"I haven't hanged a single person since I've been here," said Martin.

"I'm surprised to learn it," said Robin. "You administer the place so badly that I would have thought there'd be a hanging every week."

To hear them, you would think they loathed each other, but in actual fact they were the closest of friends.

A Question of Promotion

In such a tight little European community you had to learn to live with those people of your own color and build up a rapport with them. This was not a color bar. It was simply that at that time the numerous highly intelligent Africans who visited or lived in Mamfe would not have wished to mix with the white community because they would have felt, with their extraordinary sensitivity, that there would be embarrassment on both sides.

I felt it was high time to call the meeting to order. So, seizing a beer bottle, I banged it on the table. A chorus of "Yes, sah," "Coming, sah," came from the kitchen.

"That's the first sensible thing you've done since I arrived," said Robin.

Pious appeared carrying a tray of liquid sustenance and when all our glasses had been replenished I said, "I now call this meeting to order."

"Dear me," said Robin mildly, "how dictatorial."

"The point is," I said, "that although we all know Martin is a splendid sort of chap in his way, he is an extremely bad D.O. and, even worse, has no social graces whatsoever."

"I say," said Martin plaintively.

"I think that's a very fair assessment," said Robin.

"I think you're being *very* cruel to Martin," said Mary. "I think he's a *very* good D.O."

"Anyway," I said hastily, "we won't go into that. The reason for this council of war is so that, while Martin is making sure his district is in order, we can take over the entertainment side so there's no hitch and the whole thing runs smoothly. Now, I have inspected the house and I've got Pious in control of Martin's staff for a start."

"There are times," said McGrade, "when you have strange flourishes of genius which I can only attribute to the tiny drop of Irish blood you've got in your veins. I've long envied you that steward."

"Well, envy away," I said. "You're not pinching him from me. He's too valuable. It now comes to a question of food. And this is where I thought that Mary could help."

Mary glowed like a rosebud.

"Oh, but of course," she said. "I'll do anything. What have you got in mind?"

"Martin," I said, "I assume that he's only here for one day so we only have three meals to consider. What time will he be arriving?"

"I should think probably about seven or eight o'clock," said Martin.

"Right," I said, "what do you suggest, Mary?"

"Well, the avocados are absolutely perfect at the moment," said Mary. "And if you stuffed them with shrimps and did a sort of mayonnaise sauce which I've got the recipe for. . ."

"Mary, dear," interrupted Robin, "I have no tinned shrimps in the store and if you think I'm going to spend the next two days wading round in the river with a shrimp net, being attacked by hippos, you've got another think coming."

"Well, let's just settle on avocados," I said. "Does he like tea or coffee?"

"I don't really know," said Martin. "You see, the last time we didn't get on very intimate terms and so I couldn't find out his preferences,"

"Well then, provide both tea and coffee," I said.

"And then," said Mary excitedly, "something simple – scrambled eggs."

Martin solemnly wrote this down on his pad.

"That should keep him going for a bit," I said. "I suppose you have to show him round the place and so on?"

"Yes," said Martin, "that's all organized."

We all leaned forward and peered into his face earnestly.

"Are you sure?" I inquired.

"Oh yes, yes," said Martin. "Honestly, I've got everything organized from that point of view. It's just this bloody entertaining business."

"Well, presumably he'll want to go and look at some of the outlying areas?" I inquired.

"Oh yes," said Martin, "he always likes to poke his nose in everywhere."

"Well then, I suggest a picnic lunch. After all, if you have a picnic lunch you don't expect the Ritz standards, do you?"

"As in this remote place," said Robin, "we spend our lives living on picnic lunches and dinners and breakfasts, I don't think it would come as a great surprise to him."

"I'll do the picnic lunch," said Mary. "I'll get a haunch of goat and you can have that cold. And I think there are two lettuces that I can give you. That poor dear boy forgot to water them for four days and so I've lost almost all of them but I think these two will be all right. They're a little withered but at least they're lettuce."

Martin wrote this solemnly down on his pad. "And for afters?" he asked, looking up anxiously.

"Why not sour-sour?" I suggested. This was an extraordinary fruit that looked like a large, deformed melon with knobs on, the contents of which were white and pulpy but, whipped up and served, it had a delicious lemony sort of flavor which was very refreshing.

"Wonderful," said Mary, "what a good idea."

"Well, that's taken care of breakfast and lunch,"

I said. "Now we come to dinner and I think this is the most important thing. I've discovered that Martin has got a very elegant dining room."

"Martin's got a dining room?" said McGrade.

"Yes," I said, "an extremely elegant one."

"Well, why is it then," asked McGrade, "on the rare occasions when this parsimonious bastard asks us up here to chop, we're forced to eat on the veranda like a set of gipsy Protestants?"

"Never mind the why's and wherefore's," I said, "come and look at it."

We all trooped in solemnly and examined the dining room. I was glad to see that in the interim – though how he had found time for it I didn't know – Pious had had the table and chairs polished so that they glowed. Peering at the table top you could see your face reflected in it as though you were looking into a brown pool of water.

"Oh, but it's delicious," said Mary. "Martin, you never told us you had a room like this."

"It's certainly a marvelous table," said McGrade, bashing his enormous fist down on it so that I feared that it would split in two.

"But you can have a simply splendid dinner here," said Mary. "What an *absolutely* marvelous setting. I only wish we had some candelabras."

I was just about to suggest that she not complicate the issue when Robin unexpectedly said, "I have four."

We all looked at him in complete astonishment.

"Well, they're not silver or anything as posh as that," he said, "but they are rather nice brass ones that I bought up in Kano. They need a bit of polishing, but I think they'd look pretty good."

"Oh splendid," said Mary, her eyes shining. "Dinner by candlelight. He couldn't resist that."

"If an honest Irish Catholic is allowed to get a word in edgeways with a lot of jabbering heathens," said McGrade, "could I ask you all a question?"

We all looked at him expectantly.

"Where are we going to get the candles?"

"Dear, yes, I didn't think of that," said Mary. "You can't very well have candelabras without candles."

"I don't know why it is that people always tend to underestimate my intelligence," said Robin. "I bought the candelabras because I liked them and I intended to use them. The house I'm occupying at the moment doesn't lend itself to such medieval splendor but I did, however, take the precaution of importing a considerable quantity of candles which have been steadily melting away in a cupboard since I was moved to Mamfe. If they have not congealed into a solid mass, we might be able to salvage one or two. However, leave that part of the thing to me."

Knowing Robin as we did, we knew that the candles would not be the horrid sticky mess that he implied, for I was sure he would have checked on them four times a day.

"Well now, Mary," I said, "will you do the flower arrangements?"

"Flower arrangements?" said Martin, startled.

"But of course," I said, "a few bunches of begonias or something hung around the place always tart it up a bit."

"Well, it's rather difficult," said Mary, "at the moment. There's not really much in bloom. There's hibiscus, of course. . . ."

"Holy Mary," said McGrade, "we're surrounded by bloody hibiscus all the time. That's not a flower arrangement. That's just bringing the bloody jungle into the house."

"Well," I said, "I've got a hunter who's extremely good at climbing trees, and the other day, as well as bringing me some animals, he brought me a rather beautiful orchid which he'd got from the top of a tree. I'll contact him and get him to go out into the forest and see what orchids and other things he can get. And then, Mary dear, you do the flower arrangements."

"Oh, I love arranging flowers," said Mary, "and if they are orchids it will be absolutely marvelous."

Martin scribbled frantically on his pad.

"Now," I said to him, "what have we got organized so far?"

"Well," he said, "we've checked on the beds and furniture, we've got the staff under control, we've organized the breakfast. Mary is organizing the picnic lunch and the flower arrangements and that's really as far as we've got."

"Drinks," I said.

"I wouldn't worry about that," said Robin. "Being in charge of the only emporium that supplies you with the stuff, I know that Martin is a complete dipsomaniac and I could tell you almost down to the last bottle how much he's got here."

He glanced down into his empty glass pensively.

"Parsimoniousness is a thing that I could never suffer gladly," he added.

"Oh, for God's sake, shut up," said Martin. "If you want another drink, call Amos."

"Hush, children," I said, "let's go back onto the veranda and, raising our voices above the mating cries of the hippos, let us discuss the most important thing."

We trooped back onto the veranda, refilled our glasses, and sat for a brief moment listening to the lovely sounds of the African forest at night. Fireflies as green as emeralds were flashing past us, cicadas and crickets were playing complicated Bach melodies, and occasionally there would be a belch, a grunt, or a roar from the hippos at the bottom of the gorge.

"If I've understood your devious, heathen, Protestant mind correctly," said McGrade, draining his glass and putting it on the table in the obvious expectation that somebody would refill it for him, "I take it that what you consider to be the most important thing is the dinner in the evening."

"Yes," said Martin and I simultaneously.

In an outpost as remote as Mamfe when anybody as exalted as the D.C. came, it was automatic that all the white residents were invited to dinner.

"This is where I thought Mary would come into her own," I said.

"Oh yes," said Mary, "now here I *can* be of some help. Do you think four or five courses?"

"Holy Mary," said McGrade, "with that indolent Protestant in charge of the stores, how the hell do you think we are going to get enough for five courses?"

"Leaving aside the rather offensive Catholic attack upon me," said Robin, "I must admit that as the river is at its lowest ebb and the boat hasn't managed to get through, I am rather short of supplies. However, if McGrade is going to come to this dinner, I suggest we simply give him a plate of boiled sweet potatoes, which is, I believe, the diet on which most Irish Catholics are reared."

"Are you suggesting, then, that I am obese?" said McGrade.

"No, just obscene," said Robin.

I banged my bottle on the table. "I call the convention to order," I said. "We do not at this juncture want to discuss the physical attributes or failings of anyone. We are discussing a menu."

"Well," said Mary, "I think we ought to start with an entry."

"In France," said Robin, "they generally describe it as an entrée, which can be taken both ways, if you see what I mean."

"No, no," said Mary, "what I mean is that we ought to start off with something succulent to . . . to titillate the palate."

"Dear God," said McGrade, "I've been here now three years and I haven't had anything titillated, least of all my palate."

"But if you're going to have candelabras and things," said Mary, "you've got to have the food to go with it."

"Love of my life," said McGrade, "I agree with you entirely. But as there isn't the food here, I don't see really how you can go about producing five courses when that inefficient bastard from the United Africa Company has got his boat grounded and has probably only got a couple of tins of baked beans."

I could see that the situation was getting out of hand so I banged again with my bottle. There was another chorus of "Yes, sah" from the kitchen and more beer was produced.

"Let's settle on three courses," I said, "and let's make them as simple as possible."

"Well, the first one," said Mary excitedly, "could be a soufflé."

"Jesus can't do soufflés," said Martin.

"Who?" asked Mary, astonished.

"Jesus, my cook," Martin explained.

"I never knew that your cook was called Jesus," said

McGrade. "Why didn't you let the world know he'd risen again?"

"Well, he's risen in the most extraordinary shape," said Robin, "as a nine-foot-six Hausa with heavily indentated tribal marks on his cheeks, looks as though he's ready for the grave, and cooks appallingly."

"That's what I meant," said Martin, "so we can't have soufflés."

"What about a spot of venison?" said Robin, looking at me interrogatively.

"Although I wish to help Martin," I said, "I have no intention of killing off any of my baby duiker in order to give the D.C. venison."

"How about poached eggs on toast?" suggested McGrade, who was now on his fifth bottle of beer and not really concentrating on the important matter at hand.

"I don't think somehow that that's really posh enough," said Mary. "You know, D.C.'s like to be cosseted."

"I tell you what," I said, "have you ever tried smoked porcupine?"

"No," they all said in unison.

"Well, it's delicious if it's done properly. And I have a hunter who's constantly bringing me porcupines which he hopes I will buy from him, but as they are caught in those awful steel snares, they are always too badly damaged. I buy them and put them out of their misery and feed the meat to my animals. However, occasionally I send a bunch of them down to an old boy I know called Joseph – this is beginning to resemble an ecclesiastical conference – and he smokes the porcupine over special wood and herbs which he refuses to reveal to me. The result is quite delicious."

"You Protestant swine," said McGrade. "You've been concealing this from us."

"Only because there's not enough porcupine to go around," I said. "However, I had two brought in today that had been so badly savaged by the trap that I had to kill them. I was going to feed them to my animals but in view of this dire emergency I could send them down to Joseph and have them smoked and we could then have them on toast for what Mary so prettily calls the entry."

"I'm becoming more and more convinced," said McGrade, "that you've got real Irish blood in you. I think it's a masterly idea."

"But you can't give the D.C. porcupine," said Mary in horror.

"Mary dear," I said, "you don't tell him it's porcupine. You tell him it's venison. It's so subtly smoked that anybody who's got a palate like a D.C. could not possibly tell the difference."

Martin now checked his notebook.

"Well," he said, "what are we going to have for afters?"

"I do wish you wouldn't keep using that vulgar phrase," said Robin. "It takes me straight back to Worthing, where I had the misfortune of being brought up. What you mean is 'What are we going to have for the next two courses?'"

"I do wish you wouldn't keep picking on him," said Mary. "We're here to help him."

Robin raised his glass in solemn salute to Mary.

"Saint Mary, I am devoted to you for many reasons, the principal one being that I want to plumb, before we part company, the depths of your ignorance."

"Really, you men are so stupid," said Mary crossly.

A Question of Promotion

"I thought we were supposed to be discussing what else we were going to eat."

"Can we work on the assumption," said McGrade, "that he will probably die after the smoked porcupine and so it's not worth considering the other two courses?"

"No, no," said Martin, taking him literally, "we must have something else to follow."

"A wake," said McGrade, "there's nothing like a good Irish wake for getting everybody in a mood of frivolity."

"Now, look. Shut up and listen to me," I said. "We start with some smoked porcupine. I then suggest groundnut chop."

Everybody groaned.

"But we *always* have groundnut chop," said Robin. "It's the one thing we all live on. It's our *staple diet*."

"No, no," said Martin excitedly, "that's the reason I bought Jesus's hat."

The others, this not having been explained to them, looked slightly puzzled.

"You mean he makes a really good groundnut chop?" I inquired.

"Yes," said Martin, "best I've ever tasted *anywhere*."

Groundnut chop can only be described as a sort of Irish stew made with whatever meat is available and covered in a heavy sauce of crushed peanuts, served with a whole mass of tiny side dishes which the Africans called "small, small tings." It could be delicious or it could be a disaster.

"Well, if Jesus can do the groundnut chop," I said, "Pious is awfully good at doing the small, small tings. So that settles that as the main course."

"So what confection can we have as a sweet?" inquired Robin.

We thought about it for a moment and then looked at each other. "I think we'll have to fall back on the old stand-by," said Mary despairingly.

"I know," said McGrade, "flute salad."

Flute salad was an inevitable part of our diet. It was owing to the Cameroonians' inability to pronounce an *f* and an *r* together that it was called flute salad.

"Yes, I suppose it will have to be," said Robin dismally.

"There are several quite nice fruits at the moment," said Mary. "We could make something rather special."

"Excellent," I said, "now the whole thing is settled."

"Then drinks and coffee on the veranda and we'll get the old bastard into bed as quickly as possible," said McGrade.

"I do hope," said Martin earnestly, "that you will not drink too much and become your unpleasant Irish self. That could undo the whole evening."

"I shall be a model of propriety," said McGrade. "You'll be able to see my halo very clearly shining over my head as I tell him about all the bridges that have fallen down and all the roads that need to be repaired."

"Don't say anything like that," said Martin. "After all, I will have just been showing him how beautifully the place is run."

"One often wonders," said Robin pensively, "how England ever kept her Empire going if the English carried on in the imbecilic way that we have been carrying on tonight. Anyway, I'm going back to chop and to attend to my candelabras."

He got to his feet and wandered off, then suddenly re-materialized.

"By the way," he said, "I haven't got a white tie and tails. Does it really matter?"

A Question of Promotion

"Oh no," said Martin, "no, no, but come in a jacket and tie, and after the first five minutes we'll all get so hot we'll have to take them off anyway. Just as long as you *come* in them, that's the important thing."

Oh, God, I thought. The only tie I possessed at that time was sitting in a suitcase some three hundred miles away. Still, that was a minor problem, which I dealt with the following morning.

When Pious brought me my sustaining early morning cup of tea and I had removed one squirrel, four mongooses, and a baby chimpanzee from my bed – which they shared with me, from their point of view, out of love and affection but from my point of view simply because I didn't want them to catch chills – I told Pious to go down to the market and buy me a tie.

"Yes, sah," he said, and, having organized the rest of the staff about their duties, he strutted off into town to return some time later with a tie that was so psychedelic that I felt it would have a detrimental effect on the D.C.'s eyesight. However, Pious assured me that it was the quietest tie in the market and I had to take his word for it.

Needless to say, the next couple of days were very trying on everybody's nerves. McGrade, being very proud of his roads and bridges, had noticed to his horror that the drive up to Martin's house had several large potholes in it and so he had borrowed all the convicts from the local jail to fill these in and re-gravel the whole drive so that the entrance began to look like a medium-sized but extremely elegant country house. I had gone down to see my old man, Joseph, and persuaded him to smoke the two porcupines for me, and I also contacted my hunter who promised that the day before the D.C.'s arrival he would go into the forest and get what flowers he could. Robin had ransacked the United Africa Company's stores but was in despair at not being able to produce anything of real merit, for the boat had been unable to go up-river and he was running low on the sort of esoteric delicacies that we thought worthy of a D.C. However, his pride was immense when he announced to us that he had discovered – and God knows why they were there in the first place – three small tins of caviar which were left over from his predecessor.

"I don't know what they'll be like," he said, looking at them glumly. "They must have been here at least three years. We'll probably all die of ptomaine poisoning, but anyway it's caviar."

Mary, having discovered that Martin's house did not contain a single vase for flower arrangements, had very cleverly gone down to the market and bought five rather elegant calabashes. She had also worked out fifteen ways of trying to make soufflés with the aid of Jesus, all of which were totally impracticable and which we had to crush unmercifully underfoot.

As Pious was spending most of his time up at Martin's house, I felt sure that he would do the job perfectly, even if it meant assaulting Jesus.

The evening before the D.C.'s arrival we had another council of war to check on all our various activities, and everything appeared to be running like clockwork. The porcupines had been smoked and smelt delicious even though they were uncooked. My hunter friend had come back with an enormous array of forest orchids and plants, which Mary was keeping in her lavatory as it was the coolest part of her house. As an experiment, we opened one of the tins of caviar and it proved to our surprise to be edible, and Robin had also unearthed a packet of small biscuits. This, together with peanuts, we felt, would be suitable for the drinks before dinner. Robin's candelabras turned out to be extremely elegant pieces of brass-work, polished and gleaming, that would grace any dining room. I coveted them myself. He also had a sufficient number of candles, as McGrade sagely observed, to light up the whole of Vatican City.

We had all thrown ourselves into these tasks, partly because of our affection for Martin but also rather like children at Christmas time. I was probably the only one who had any excitement each day, because I never knew what strange habit I might observe among my animals but, by and large, the others led very dull, routine lives in a most unpleasant climate. So, although we all pretended that the arrival of the D.C. was a terrible bore and kept piling curses on his head, we all rather enjoyed ourselves. That is, with the exception of Martin, who looked more and more shaky as the day approached.

When the fateful day actually arrived we were all quite casually standing under a sour-sour tree which commanded a very convenient view of the entrance to Martin's residence. We all talked nervously about animal behavior, the rising cost of manufactured cloth, and the difficulty of building a bridge, and Mary gave us a long lecture on the art of cookery. Nobody listened to anybody else for we were waiting with bated breath for the arrival of the D.C.

At last, to our immense relief, his large and rather elegant car arrived, swept up the drive, and came to a halt in front of the house.

"By God, those pot-holes held," said McGrade. "I was worried about them."

We saw Martin come out and the D.C. emerged from his car. From a distance he looked like a small caterpillar emerging from a large black cocoon. Martin looked immaculate. Then he ushered the D.C. into the house and we all heaved sighs of relief.

"I'm *sure* he'll like the avocados," said Mary. "Do you know I went through forty-three of them to pick out the best."

"And my pot-holes held," said McGrade proudly. "Takes an Irishman to do a job like that."

"You wait till he gets to the caviar," said Robin. "That, as far as I'm concerned, will be the high point of the evening."

"What about my smoked porcupine?" I said indignantly.

"And what about my flower arrangements?" said Mary. "One would think that you'd done everything, Robin."

"Well, I have, virtually," said Robin. "I have contributed my brain."

Then we all went our separate ways to our late breakfasts. We could do nothing further until the evening. The rest was in Martin's hands and we knew that, being the person that he was, the D.C. would find very little wrong in the way Martin was handling the district.

At five o'clock Pious materialized at my elbow just as I had been bitten in the thumb by an indignant pouched rat whom I had been inspecting to see whether she was pregnant.

"Sah," said Pious.

"Na whatee?" I asked, sucking the blood off my thumb.

"Barf ready, sah."

"Why the hell are you passing me a bath at this time of the day?" I asked, having completely forgotten what a momentous occasion it was.

A Question of Promotion

Pious looked at me with surprise. "You got to be at D.O.'s for six o'clock, sah," he said.

"Damn," I said, "I'd forgotten all about it. Have you organized my clothes?"

"Yes, sah," said Pious. "Small boy has ironed your trousers. Clean shirt, sah. Your jacket is ready and your tie."

"God in Heaven," I said, suddenly struck by a thought, "I don't think I've brought any socks with me."

"I buy you socks, sah, for market, sah," said Pious. "I done clean your shoes."

Reluctantly leaving my investigations, I went and had my bath, in a sort of canvas coffin full of lukewarm water. In spite of this and in spite of the hour of the day, I was dripping with sweat and bath water in equal quantities. I flopped into a chair in a vague endeavor to cool off and thought about the evening that stretched before me. The thought was so appalling that it made me shudder.

"Pious," I shouted.

"Sah," he said.

"Pass me a drink," I said.

"Beer, sah?"

"No," I said, "a very big whisky with water."

I drank this sustaining liquid and began to feel in a merrier mood. I dressed with care, though because of the heat and the sweat, the beautifully laundered pearl-white shirt became grey and damp almost immediately. The socks that Pious had purchased for me were apparently the hunting colors of one of the remoter Scottish clans and clashed abominably with my tie. I did not put on my jacket but slung it over my shoulder, for I knew that if I wore my jacket for the short climb up to Martin's house, I would end up meeting the D.C. looking like a seal newly emerged from the ocean. Pious walked up with me.

"Are you sure everything's all right?" I asked.

"Yes, sah," he said. "But the D.O.'s boys, sah, they not really good boys."

"I know that," I said. "That's why I put you in charge."

"Yes, sah. Please, sah, Jesus goes funny."

Dear God, I thought, what can happen now? "What do you mean, he goes funny?"

"He's a good man," said Pious earnestly, "but he's an old man and so when he go make dis sort of ting he go funny."

"You mean he gets frightened?" I asked.

"Yes, sah," said Pious.

"So you think he might make a bad chop?"

"Yes, sah," said Pious.

"Well, what are we going to do about that?" I asked.

"I done send our cook up, sah," said Pious. "'E go help Jesus and then Jesus go be all right."

"Good," I said, "a very good idea."

Pious beamed with pride. We walked on for a bit in silence.

"Please, sah."

"Whatee?" I asked irritably.

"I send our small boy too, sah," said Pious. "Dat small boy is good boy but Amos never teach um."

"Excellent," I said, "I'll have you recommended for the New Year's Honours List."

"Tank you, sah," said Pious, not understanding but judging from the way I spoke that these decisions that he had made on his own met with my full support.

When we got to Martin's place Pious, who had done himself up in his best uniform – for which I had paid an exorbitant amount of money and added brass buttons too, and which he had so seldom an opportunity to display – de-materialized from my elbow and disappeared in the direction of the kitchen.

The front door was open and on one side of it stood my own small boy. His shorts and tunic had been laundered and ironed with such care that they looked like a Swiss ski slope before the beginning of a season.

"Iseeya, sah," he said, beaming at me.

"Iseeya, Ben," I said, "and make sure that you work hard tonight or I go kill you tomorrow."

"Yes, sah," he said smiling.

I found that, owing to my dilatoriness in taking a slow bath, a slow whisky, and a slow and reluctant entry into clothes that were totally unsuitable for the climate, the others had arrived before me and were all sitting on the veranda.

"Ahhh," said Martin, leaping to his feet and coming to greet me, "I thought perhaps you weren't coming."

"Dear boy," I whispered, "I would not let you down in your hour of need."

"Let me introduce you," he said, pushing me into the crowd on the veranda. "Mr. Featherstone Hugh, the District Commissioner."

He was a smallish man whose face closely resembled a badly made pork pie. He had thinning grey hair and very pale blue but penetrating eyes. He rose from his chair and shook hands with me, and his handshake was surprisingly strong because he looked at first glance to be rather a vapid sort of man, the sort one would have thought had got on by being a political animal rather than a sensitive and intuitive one.

"Ah, Durrell," he said, "delighted to meet ye."

"I'm so sorry I'm late, sir," I said.

"Not at all, not at all," he said. "Sit ye down. I'm sure Bugler here has the odd drink hidden away which he can give you, eh, Bugler?"

"Oh, yes, yes, yes, sir," said Martin. He clapped his hands and a chorus of "Yes, sah's" came from the kitchen. To my relief Pious appeared, with his brass buttons glittering in the lamplight.

"Sah?" he said to me as though he had never met me before.

"Whisky and water," I said, adopting the cold attitude that so many people used towards their servants. I felt that coming from Nigeria the D.C. would appreciate my falling into the right sort of British habits. I took a swift glance round at the circle of faces. Mary, round-eyed, was hanging on the D.C.'s every word. If she had had a neon sign above her head saying "I hope for a promotion for my husband" it couldn't have been more obvious. Robin gave me a swift glance, raised his eyebrows, and then went into one of his dream-like trances. McGrade had a rather smug look on his face and beamed at me benevolently.

The long couch on the veranda was littered with coats and ties and there was a semi-cool breeze blowing up from the river.

"Excuse me, sir," I said, to the D.C., "do you mind if I adopt the local custom and take off my tie and jacket?"

"Of course, of course," said the D.C. "All informal here. I was just explaining to Bugler here. Really a matter of routine. Just come through once or twice a year to keep an eye on you chaps. Make sure you're not getting up to any mischief."

With infinite relief I removed my jacket and my rainbow-colored tie and flung them on the couch. Pious passed me my drink, for which I did not thank him.

Generally it was not done to thank your servants for anything in West Africa. Nor did you call them by their Christian names. You simply clapped your hands and shouted, "Boy."

The conversation had come to a complete halt during this operation. It was quite obvious that the D.C. was holding the floor and that nobody else could speak until he did. I sipped my drink reflectively and wondered what on earth I could have in common with the D.C. and indeed whether I was going to survive the evening with my mental faculties intact.

"Chin, chin," said the D.C. as I raised the glass to my lips.

"Your very good health, sir," I said.

The D.C. settled himself more comfortably in his chair, adjusted his glass on the arm of it, glanced round to see that he had a rapt audience, and then began.

"As I was saying, Durrell, just before your late arrival, I'm extremely pleased that Bugler here has got this place apparently in perfect order. As you know, we chaps have to potter out occasionally just to make sure that the various areas *are* kept in order." Here he gave the most uncharming chuckle and drank deeply from his glass.

"Awfully good of you to say so, sir," said Martin.

He then saw Mary turning imploring, anguished eyes upon him.

"But, of course," he added hastily, "I couldn't have done it without the aid of a splendid A.D.O."

"I think you're being too modest, Bugler," said the D.C. "After all, A.D.O.'s can be a help or a hindrance."

"Oh, but I assure you that Standish is absolutely marvelous," said Martin, making one of his sweeping gestures and knocking the large bowl of roasted peanuts into the D.C.'s lap.

"Sorry, sah," came a chorus from Pious, Amos, and the two small boys, who were standing waiting in the shadows like hunting dogs. They converged upon the D.C. and while muttering "Sorry, sah," "Sorry, sah," they swept the greasy peanuts from his clean trousers back into the bowl and removed it to the kitchen.

"I'm terribly, terribly sorry, sir," said Martin.

"Oh, it's just an accident," said the D.C., looking at the grease stains on his trousers. "*Could* happen to anyone. But I must say you do seem to go in for this sort of thing, what? Where was that place I visited you?"

"Yes, and I'm awfully sorry about that," said Martin, interrupting hurriedly, "but it was a complete misunderstanding you understand, sir. I assure you the lavatory here works perfectly."

McGrade, Robin, and Mary looked completely and utterly mystified by this conversation.

"Yes, well, as I was saying," said the D.C., glancing down again at the oil stains on his pants, "I think that Bugler has done a very good job."

He paused and drank.

"And of course," he said, as an afterthought, leaning forward and bowing sanctimoniously to Mary, "aided by you and your husband, Bugler seems to have done awfully well. The roads and bridges seem to be in remarkably fine fettle." He glanced at McGrade.

"Thank you, sir," said McGrade with mock civility.

"And I understand," continued the D.C., addressing Robin, "although of course your chops don't come under us chaps, that you managed to provide this excellent caviar. Remarkable to find such a thing in Mamfe."

Robin gave a little bow. "I deeply *appreciate* your *appreciation*," he said, "for as you well know, sir, caviar comes from the virgin sturgeon."

146

"I think the whole thing is absolutely splendid," said the D.C. "As a matter of fact, it is one of the best tours I've had so far, but don't let it go any further, for it might hurt certain people's feelings. Ha ha!"

We all laughed dutifully. I was watching the level of the gin in the D.C.'s glass because I had planned things with Pious, knowing that this sort of conversation could not go on interminably without driving us all mad. So at the precise moment that the D.C. drained the last drops from his glass, Pious appeared, all polished buttons, and said to Martin, "Jesus say chop ready, sah."

"Ah, chop," said the D.C., slapping his stomach, "just what we all need, don't you agree, little lady?" He gave Mary a rather arch glance.

"Oh, yes," said Mary, flustered, "I think chop is awfully important, especially in this climate."

"Actually," said Robin, as we all got to our feet and walked towards the dining room, "I have always been under the biological impression that chop was important in any climate."

Fortunately the D.C. didn't hear this remark.

Martin seized me by the shoulder and whispered frenziedly in my ear, "What about seating?"

"Put Mary at one end of the table and the D.C. at the other."

"Oh, good," he said. "And I've done something rather clever."

"Oh, God," I said, "what have you done now?"

"No, no," he said, "it's perfectly all right. But while you all were being so helpful I felt I had to contribute in some sort of way. I've got the punkah to work and Amos's son is out there to pull on the cord so at least we'll have some fresh air in the room."

"We're obviously having a good effect on you, Martin,"

I said. "By the time we've finished with you, you'll be able to socialize like mad. Now go on ahead and make sure that everybody sits where they're supposed to sit."

"The awful thing is we're uneven numbers," said Martin.

"Never mind," I said, "as long as we get Mary at one end of the table and the D.C. at the other, you can spread the rest of us to look like a crowd."

I must say the dining room looked extremely impressive. The table and chairs glowed in the candlelight like freshly husked chestnuts. Three candelabras ran down the centre of the table and the fourth was on the massive sideboard. Pious had done his job well. The cutlery and the china gleamed in the candlelight. If the D.C. wasn't impressed by this, I thought, nothing would impress him.

We sat down and Pious, who had obviously got Amos and the small boy, John, under control, passed drinks of our choice.

"By Jove," said the D.C., glancing at the shining candelabras, the polished table, and the gently swinging punkah, "you're very well placed here, Bugler, aren't you? Positive Government House, what?"

"No, no, sir," said Martin hastily, obviously under the impression the D.C. thought he was spending too much money. "We don't always eat like this. Normally we eat sort of bush fashion, if you know what I mean. But we felt this was a special occasion."

"Quite right," said the D.C., "I understand perfectly."

Pious, with all the deference and decorum of a head waiter from Claridge's, served small square chunks of porcupine on pieces of crisp toast.

"By Jove," said the D.C., "what's this?"

Martin, who by this time was in an acute state of

nerves, was just about to say, "porcupine," when Mary, in her calm, placid voice, said, "Once you've eaten it we want you to guess. It's a surprise."

The porcupine, as I knew it would be, was excellent. The D.C. engulfed it with obvious enjoyment.

"Ha!" he said as he swallowed the last mouthful, "you can't catch me – venison! Eh, what?"

The look of relief on Martin's face almost gave the whole thing away but again Mary stepped into the breach.

"But how clever of you," she said. "We thought you'd never recognize it since it's been smoked and prepared in a special way."

"Can't catch me out on things like that," said the D.C., preening himself. "Don't forget I was an A.D.O. once and had to live in the bush and live rough. We used to feed off all sorts of things. These local antelopes are unmistakable, but I must admit this has been wonderfully smoked."

"As a matter of fact," I said, "it's a thing that we do have occasionally and Martin was clever enough to find a small man down the road who has a special recipe for smoking and does it extremely well. So on the very rare occasions when we manage to get the venison, Martin is kind enough to distribute some to us so we can all enjoy it."

While this rather tricky conversation had been going on, the enormous platter of groundnut chop had been placed in front of Mary, and down the long shining table had appeared some twenty little plates containing the small, small tings. It really looked most impressive.

"I'm sorry, sir, we can't think of anything except groundnut chop," said Martin, who had an awful tendency to apologize in advance, thus giving his adversary a chance to complain. "But normally my cook does it frightfully well."

"I know one tends to eat too much of it," said the D.C., "but, really, I think it's a very good, sustaining food."

Mary had served the groundnut chop with rice onto the plates, which were solemnly carried by Amos and Pious and distributed among us. Then came the sort of chess game that one has to play with the small, small tings.

The D.C.'s plate was piled high. He added three or four chunks of pink pawpaw and looked at it with satisfaction.

"Splendid," he said, "it looks absolutely splendid."

Martin began to look a little less strained, for he knew that my cook was helping Jesus and that the groundnut chop would probably be excellent.

Mary, on her best behavior, looked at the D.C., who gravely bowed his head, and she dipped her spoon and fork into the groundnut chop. The D.C. followed suit and then we all picked up our implements and attacked our plates. The punkah, creaking slightly, waved to and fro and sent wafts of warm air upon us.

"Best groundnut chop I've ever had," said the D.C., having just swallowed an enormous mouthful.

Martin beamed at me across the table.

"Martin's a great one for organizing," said McGrade.

"Indeed he is. I agree with you entirely," said Robin. "I fear that on this occasion it is I who have failed."

"Failed?" said the D.C. "How d'ye mean, failed?"

"Well, we could have put on a much more splendiferous meal for you," said Robin, "but unfortunately the river ran rather dry and the boat with the supplies couldn't get up. So I'm afraid poor Martin's doing the best he can in the circumstances."

"Yes," said Mary, "we'd hoped to put on a really *good* meal for you."

"Nonsense, nonsense," said the D.C., waving his hands deprecatingly. "This is superb."

Martin positively glowed and relaxed.

"Tell me," said the D.C., "I understand you're an animal collector, Durrell."

"Yes, sir," I answered.

"But surely you don't find much around here?" he inquired.

During the course of our drinks on the veranda I had seen Pious swiftly and silently remove a praying mantis and a gecko from the D.C.'s chair.

"When I was an A.D.O.," he said, "wandering about in the bush, never saw a damn thing."

"Oh, there's an amazing amount of stuff around here if you know where to look for it, sir," I said. "Why, only the other day I caught quite a rare creature at the bottom of Martin's garden. There's plenty of life here if you look for it."

"Extraordinary," said the D.C., shovelling a great spoonful of groundnut chop into his mouth. "I wouldn't have thought there was anything living so near to civilization, as it were."

At that moment came a noise like somebody breaking the backbone of a whale, and with a rustle like a million autumn leaves being caught by a hurricane, the palm-leaf punkah crashed straight onto the table, one end of it completely obliterating the D.C.

Fortunately, it put out the candles so that nothing caught fire, but it did, however, contain in its many ballet-skirt-like sets of fronds an extremely interesting cross-section of the local fauna that lived in close proximity to civilization.

The effect upon the party was considerable.

"Oh, my God! Oh, my God!" screamed Mary, leaping to her feet, upsetting her gin and tonic and losing her normal pose of placidity.

"Why didn't you let me check it, you stupid bastard!" roared McGrade.

"There are times when I really despair of you, Martin," said Robin with some asperity.

"I'm terribly, terribly sorry, sir," said Martin to the invisible D.C. "I really don't know how to apologize."

He was trembling from head to foot at the catastrophe.

The palm fronds rustled and the D.C.'s head appeared. He emerged from the punkah looking not unlike an albino African emerging from his hut. He opened his mouth to say something and then caught sight of a chocolate-colored, very hairy spider the circumference of a saucer making its way along the punkah towards him. Already the rich and happy little community that had been living in the fan undisturbed for years was starting to emerge. The D.C. pushed back his chair and leapt to his feet.

I knew this was a disaster of the worst sort from Martin's point of view, but I have always found in life that one should seize every opportunity. It seemed as though the punkah was going to provide me with some interesting specimens.

"I suggest you all go into the other room," I said, noticing a new species of gecko emerging from the palm fronds. "I'll fix things in here."

The parts of the table that were still visible were rapidly becoming covered with indignant beetles and other specimens of lesser life, who looked, even if they were not, extremely malevolent.

Mary pulled herself together and with great grace led the way out of the dining room and onto the veranda and the others trooped after her.

The staff had been frozen solid because, as we had been sitting in our chairs, it would have been extremely difficult to remove the palm-leaf fan and pretend that dinner was going on as normal. It was a situation they had not met with before and even Pious was incapable of coping with it.

"Pious," I roared, startling him out of his horrified trance, "go bring bottles, boxes, anything for catch this beef."

Beef is the all-important West African term meaning any animal that walks, flies, or crawls. Pious, grabbing Amos and the two small boys by the scruff of the neck, disappeared.

By this time a number of other interesting inhabitants were appearing out of the punkah to see why their community life had been disturbed. The first to emerge was a young and highly indignant green mamba, reputedly the most deadly snake in Africa. He was about two feet long, like a green and yellow plaited lariat and you could tell from his attitude that the whole thing was very upsetting to his psyche. I tried to pin him down with a fork but he wriggled free and fell off the table onto the floor. It was only then that I realized that although all the others had fled to the veranda and left the disaster to me, the D.C. had stayed on. The green mamba, in that irritating way that snakes have, with the whole of the room to choose from, wriggled straight towards the D.C., who remained rooted to the spot, his face going a rather interesting shade of blue. I made another quick assault on the mamba and this time succeeded in pinning him down and picking him up by the back of the neck. By this time Pious had returned, having unearthed from the kitchen jars, boxes, bottles, and other containers. I slipped the green mamba into a bottle and corked it up securely.

The D.C. was still regarding me with bulging eyes. I had to say something in an attempt to cover up the disaster and protect Martin. I smiled at the D.C. beguilingly.

"You see what I mean, sir?" I said airily, removing a large beetle from the groundnut chop where he was lying on his back waving his legs and uttering shrill mechanical whirrings. "The animals are all around you. It's merely a question of finding out where they live."

He stared at me for a moment.

"Yes. Yes, I can see that," he said, adding, "I think I need a drink."

"It was extremely clever of you to stand still, sir," I said.

"Why?" asked the D.C. suspiciously.

"Well, most people in those circumstances would have panicked, sir, but you kept your head admirably. If it hadn't been for you I doubt whether I'd have ever caught the mamba."

The D.C. looked at me suspiciously again, but I was wearing my most innocent expression.

"Hah!" he said. "Well, let's go and have a drink."

"Well, I think there are one or two more creatures here for me to catch and I'd better get Martin to organize things a bit. I'll join you in a minute, sir, if I may."

"Certainly," he said. "I'll send Martin to you."

Martin staggered into the dining room looking like the sole survivor of the *Titanic*.

"Jesus Christ," he said, "I never thought. . . ."

"Look," I said firmly, "just don't think. Do what I say."

"It's worse than the lavatory!"

"Nothing could be worse than the lavatory. Now, just take things calmly."

While we were talking Pious and I were busy collecting further denizens of the fan, which consisted of numerous geckos, eight tree frogs, a hysterical dormouse with its nest and young, three bats, a couple of irascible scorpions, and an incredible number of beetles.

"What are we going to *do?*" asked Martin in despair, almost wringing his hands.

I turned to Pious and I could tell from his expression that he was as worried by this awful catastrophe as Martin was. I, unfortunately, was suffering from an almost uncontrollable desire to laugh loud and long, but I didn't dare to do so.

"Now," I said to Pious, "you go for Masa McGrade's house and you find chop. Then you go for Masa Girton's house and you find chop. Then you go for A.D.O.'s house and find chop. Then you go for our place and find chop. I want chop in one hour, you hear."

"I hear, sah," said Pious and disappeared.

"God, I shall be sent back to Umchichi," said Martin.

"That might well happen," I said, "but judging by the D.C.'s reaction it will not."

"But he couldn't have been pleased," said Martin.

"I don't think anybody was, with the possible exception of me. I've got some nice specimens out of it."

"But what are we going to do now?" asked Martin, gazing at the wreckage of the table.

I sat him down in a chair.

"I sent the D.C. to call you because I said you could control the situation," I explained. "Pious has gone to fetch the chop. What it'll be, God only knows, but at least it will be something to eat. In the meantime, you must try and fill the D.C. up with as much gin as possible."

"I've got plenty of gin," said Martin earnestly.

"Well, there you are," I said soothingly. "The problem's almost solved."

"But I don't see how. . . ." Martin said.

"Look, just don't think about it. Leave it to me. The point is, you have to appear as though you are in control of the situation."

"Oh. Yes, I see what you mean," said Martin.

I called Amos and John from the kitchen.

"Clean up this table, polish it, and put things for chop," I said.

"Yes, sah," they said in a chorus.

"Pious done go for chop. You tell Jesus and my cook they can make new chop."

"Yes, sah."

"But you go make the table look fine like before, you hear?"

"Please, sah," said Amos.

"Whatee?" I asked.

"Masa done catch all de snakes from inside dere?" inquired Amos, pointing at the wreckage of the punkah.

"Yes," I said. "You no go fear. I done catch all the beef."

"I don't know how you organize things so well," said Martin.

"Listen," I said, "as far as the D.C. is concerned, *you've* organized all this. Now, when we join them you assume an almost military pose. You've got to give the D.C. the impression that while I was more concerned with my animals you had everything else under perfect control. And don't apologize every five minutes! We'll get him well ginned up and Pious will have the food under control, so don't worry about that. All you have to do is give the impression that although this is a disaster, it is a very minor one and you are quite sure that on thinking it over the D.C. will see the funny side of it."

"The funny side of it?" said Martin faintly.

"Yes," I said. "How long have you been in the Colonial Service?"

"Since I was twenty-one," he said.

"Don't you realize that people like this pompous ass dine out on stories like this? You've probably done yourself more good than harm."

"Are you sure?" said Martin doubtfully.

"You think about it," I said. "Now let's go out onto the veranda."

So we joined the D.C. on the veranda and found that the others had been doing stalwart service. Mary had given the D.C. a long lecture on orchids and flower arrangements. McGrade had given him such a complicated discourse on bridge building and road maintenance that I don't think even *he* could have understood. And Robin had come in at just the right moment to discuss literature and art, two subjects about which the D.C. knew nothing.

I dug Martin in the ribs and he straightened up.

"I'm terribly sorry about that, sir," he said. "Most unfortunate. I'm afraid my boy didn't check on the hooks in the ceiling. However, I have ... er ... organized everything and we should have chop in about an hour. Terribly sorry to keep you waiting."

He subsided into a chair and mopped his face with his handkerchief.

The D.C. looked at him speculatively and drained his tenth gin.

"I don't usually," he said acidly, "in the course of my duties have fans dropped on my head."

There was a short but ominous silence. It was obvious that Martin could think of nothing to say, so I stepped into the breach.

"I must say, sir, that I was damned glad to have you there," I said.

I turned to the others.

"Of course, you all didn't see it but there was a mamba in that fan. If it hadn't been for the D.C., I doubt whether I would have got it."

"A mamba!" squeaked Mary.

"Yes," I said, "and he was in a very nasty mood, I can assure you. But fortunately the D.C. kept his head and so we managed to catch it."

"Well," said the D.C., "I wouldn't go so far as to say that I helped very much."

"Oh that's modesty, sir," I said. "Most people would have panicked. After all, a mamba is supposed to be the most deadly snake in Africa."

"A mamba!" said Mary. "Fancy that! Think of it, coiled there over our heads waiting to attack! I do think you were both awfully brave."

"By Jove, yes," said Robin smoothly. "I'm afraid I would have run like a hare."

"So would I," said McGrade, who was built like an all-in wrestler and not afraid of anything.

"Well," said the D.C. deprecatingly, having found himself forced into the position of hero, "you get used to this sort of situation, you know, especially when you're trekking around in the bush."

A Question of Promotion

He embarked on a long and slightly incoherent story about a leopard he had nearly shot once and we all sighed with relief when Pious emerged out of the gloom and informed us that our second dinner was ready.

Cold baked beans and tinned salmon were not what one would call a gastronomic delight, but they served their purpose and by the end of dinner, full of gin, the D.C. was telling us some most improbable snake stories.

Fortunately, the flute salad had not been within range of the catastrophe and so this had been salvaged and after we had eaten it we all agreed that Mary, who had put her heart and soul into it, had done us proud and that it was the flute salad to end all flute salads.

When we finally left I thanked the D.C. once more for his courage in helping me catch the mamba.

"Nothing, my dear fellow," he said, waving his hand airily. "Nothing, I assure you. Glad to have been of assistance."

The following day, Martin, in spite of all our efforts, was inconsolable. The D.C., he said, had been rather frosty when he left and he was convinced that his next posting would be back to the hell-hole of Umchichi. There was nothing we could do but write polite notes to the D.C. thanking him for the disastrous dinner party. I did manage to insert in mine additional thanks for the considerable help that his D.O. had given me. I said that in my experience in West Africa Martin was one of the best and most efficient D.O.'s I had come across.

Shortly after that I had to move my animals down country to catch the ship back to England and the whole incident faded from my mind.

Then, six months later, I got a brief note from Martin. In it he said, "You were quite right, old boy, about this dining out on stories stuff. The D.C. is now telling everybody how he caught a green mamba for you on the dining-room table while you were apparently so petrified with fright you couldn't do anything sensible. I've got a promotion and go to Enugu next month. I can't thank you all enough for making the dinner party such a success."

⚸ A Question of Degrees ⚸

THE FAMILY DOCTOR shook his head more in sorrow than in anger.

"Strain," he repeated. "Over-work and over-worry. What you need is three weeks in Abbotsford."

"You mean the loony bin?" I asked.

"It isn't a loony bin. It's a *highly* respectable nursing home that specializes in nervous complaints," he said severely.

"In other words a loony bin," I said.

"I thought that you would have known better," said the family doctor sadly.

"A loose generic term," I said. "Is it that sprawling Strawberry Hill Gothic edifice that looks like Dracula's castle – the thing straight out of Hollywood – on the way to Surbiton?"

"Yes, that's the place."

"Well, I don't suppose that will be so bad," I said judiciously. "I can nip up to town to see my friends and the odd show. . . ."

"You will do nothing of the sort," the family doctor interrupted firmly. "Complete rest and quiet is what you need."

"Couldn't I have a going-in party?" I pleaded.

"A going-in party?"

"Well, debs have their coming-out parties. Why can't

I have a going-in party? Just a select band of friends to wish me God-speed on my way to the padded cell."

The family doctor winced and sighed.

"You will probably have it even if I tell you not to," he said in a resigned manner, "so I suppose you can."

The party was a small one held in an excellent curry restaurant in Soho. It was during the course of the evening that I felt something trickling down my chin and, on wiping my mouth with my napkin, I was surprised to see it stained with blood. It was obvious that my nose was bleeding. Fortunately, both the lighting and the decor of the restaurant lent themselves well to this manifestation and I managed to stanch the flow without any untoward comment. I was not so lucky on the following day.

It was a week before Christmas and it was therefore necessary for me – on my way to Abbotsford – to deviate from my route slightly to call in at the Kings Road to deliver an almost life-sized Teddy bear, who squatted regally in a transparent plastic bag and wore nothing except a handsome maroon-colored tie.

I got out of the taxi, clasping the bear round its ample middle, rang the front-door bell, and my nose started to bleed copiously. It was well nigh impossible, I discovered, to hold the bear under one arm while stanching the flow of blood with the other, so I put the bear between my legs, thus freeing my hands.

"What are you *doing?*" inquired my wife from the interior of the taxi.

"By dose is bleeding again," I said through my blood-stained handkerchief.

With the bear between my legs and the blood streaming down my face, I presented an arresting sight even by Kings Road standards. A small crowd collected.

"Give the bear to the sweet shop next door and ask *them* to give it to Peter," my wife hissed. "You can't stand there like that."

The crowd had hitherto been silent, digesting this slightly macabre spectacle. Now a new woman joined them and gaped upon the mystery.

"Wot's 'appening?" she inquired of the world in general.

"'E was bit by 'is Teddy bear," said a man and the crowd laughed uproariously at the joke.

I dived into the sanctuary of the sweet shop, deposited the Teddy bear, and then rushed panting out to the taxi.

"You shouldn't rush about so," said my wife as the taxi got under way. "You're supposed to take it easy."

"How can I dake it easy?" I inquired aggrievedly, "when by bloody dose is bleeding and I'm holding a sodding great Deddy bear?"

"Just lie back and relax," said my wife soothingly.

Relax, I thought, yes, that was it, relax. I would have three glorious weeks to relax in, being ministered unto by kindly nurses, only having to make momentous decisions like what I would have for lunch or the exact temperature of my bath water. Relax, that was it. Complete peace and quiet. So, with this thought firmly in my mind, I entered Abbotsford.

I had little time to register anything (except that the furniture and decor of my room were best Seaside Boarding House, circa 1920, and that the nurses were remarkably pretty) before I was wrapped in a golden cocoon of drugs and remained thus, sleeping and twitching in this delectable hibernation, for twenty-four hours. Then I awoke, bright and brisk as a squirrel, and surveyed my new world. My first impression of the nurses

163

had not, I decided, been erroneous. They were all in their individual ways remarkably attractive. It was rather like being looked after by the entrants for a Miss World competition.

Of the day staff there were Lorraine, the Swedish blonde, whose eyes changed color like a fiord in the sun; Zena, half English and half German, who had orange hair and completely circular and perpetually astonished blue eyes; and Nelly, a charmer from Basutoland, carved out of fine milk chocolate and with a little round nose like a brown button mushroom. Then there was the night staff: Breeda, short, blonde as honey and motherly; and, without doubt the most attractive of them all, Pimmie (a nickname derived from God knows what source), who was tall, slender, and elf-like, with enormous greeny-hazel eyes the color of a trout stream in spring. They were young and cheerful and went about their work with all the gaiety and eagerness to please of a litter of puppies. Their gambollings were presided over by two Sisters, both French, whose combined accents would have made Maurice Chevalier sound as though he had been brought up at Oxford and had worked for the BBC for a number of years. These were the Sisters Louise and Renée, and their blunt French practicality in action was a pleasure to watch and to listen to.

It was on the second day, still slightly drugged, that I, partly from desire and partly from a need for new scenery, made my way down the corridor to the lavatory. Here I squatted, thinking deep thoughts, when suddenly my attention was attracted to a large blob of blood on the floor. Hello, I thought to myself, with the rapid perception of the semi-drugged, someone's cut themselves ... been bleeding. Shaving, no doubt. But, shaving here? In the lavatory? Surely not. At that moment

another blob of blood joined the first one on the floor
and I suddenly realized that my nose was bleeding again.
By the time I had grasped this, my nose was in full flood.
Clasping several yards of lavatory paper to my face,
I sped back to my room and rang the bell frantically.
My nose was now bleeding so fast that a paper hand-
kerchief applied to it became sodden and useless almost
immediately.

In answer to my *cri de cœur* the door opened and
chocolate-brown Nelly appeared, clad in an overcoat.
She was obviously just going off duty.

"Lord, man," said Nelly, gazing round-eyed at the
bloody apparition. "Lord, yo' is bleeding."

"I had come to the same conclusion," I said. "Can
you stop it for me, Nelly dear?"

"Wait now . . . don' yo' move," Nelly commanded, and
rushed off down the corridor. Presently she reappeared,
looking distinctly distraught.

"I can' fin' dem, I can' fin' dem," she said, almost
wringing her hands in despair.

"What can't you find?"

"De keys, de keys," wailed Nelly.

Presumably the keys for some cupboard containing medicament for the rapid coagulation of blood,
I thought.

"Never mind," I said soothingly, "can't we use something else?"

"No, no," said Nelly, "de keys is best for putting
down yo' back."

My hopes for the future of European medicine in
Africa suffered a severe blow at this remark.

Lorraine and Zena, attracted by the noise, appeared
in the doorway.

"You're bleeding," said Zena in astonishment.

"Yes," I said.

"I can' fin' de keys, Zena. Have yo' seen dem, Lorraine?"

"Keys? No," said Lorraine. "I haven't seen any keys. What keys?"

"To put down his back," said Nelly.

"Don't you burn feathers beneath the nose?" asked Lorraine.

"No, no, dat's for fainting," said Nelly, the expert on modern medicine.

"How about sacrificing a black cock in a chalk circle?" I asked, beginning to enjoy the situation.

"You'd never get that on National Health," said Zena judiciously and with perfect seriousness.

At that moment Breeda and Pimmie arrived to take over the night shift. Pimmie took in the situation with one searchlight-like glance from her huge, liquid eyes.

"On to the bed wit yer," she said to me. "On to the bed and lie as flat as yer can."

"But . . . I . . ." I began to protest.

"Stop yer blarney and on to the bed wit yer. Breeda, go and get me some one-inch gauze bandage and some adrenalin. Quickly now."

I lay down obediently and immediately discovered that the blood that had been running out of my nose now ran down the back of my throat and threatened to asphyxiate me. I sat up hurriedly.

"I told yer to lie down," said Pimmie ominously.

"Pimmie, dear, I *can't*. I'll choke on my own blood," I explained.

Pimmie flicked a couple of pillows behind my head with practiced ease.

"There now, is that better?" she inquired.

"Yes," I said.

Breeda had returned with a dish containing the things Pimmie had asked for. The bed was now bestrewn with blood-stained paper handkerchiefs and there were five nurses clustered round my recumbent form.

"Kiss me, Hardy," I implored, holding out my arms to Pimmie.

"Quit yer blathering," she said severely, "and let me get this up yer nose."

With great deftness she proceeded to plug my right nostril with a yard or so of bandage soaked in adrenalin as neatly and as impersonally as though she were stuffing a chicken. Then she pinched the bridge of my nose firmly between finger and thumb, at the same time applying ice to my temples. I now had trickles of blood and water soaking into my pyjamas, but very soon the blood burst through the bandage and fell in great gouts on the sheets and pillow cases. Pimmie replaced the bandage with a fresh one. The bed and the room now looked like a cross between an abattoir and the front parlor of the Marquis de Sade after a soirée. Several bandages later, the blood was still flowing merrily. By this time all the nurses with the exception of Pimmie and Breeda had departed.

"It's no good," said Pimmie, frowning ferociously. "I'll just have to tell the doctor. Lie still now. Breeda, see that he lies still."

She left the room.

"I hope she hasn't gone to get Dr. Grubbins," I said uneasily. "Charming though he is, I lack confidence in him as a doctor."

"I hope for your sake she hasn't gone to fetch him," said Breeda placidly.

"Why?" I inquired, alarmed.

"Well," said Breeda, "he's not a good doctor at all.

Honestly, if I had a patient who was ever so ill, I wouldn't call him in. He'd kill them off for sure."

"That was rather the impression I gained," I admitted. "He had a certain *je ne sais quoi* about him that led me to suppose that he had not as yet passed the stage of pouring boiling pitch over the stump."

"Ignorant," said Breeda gloomily. "He thinks pasteurization is something you do to the meadows that cows feed in."

"And that Lister is something a boat does when it's badly loaded?" I inquired, entering into the spirit of the game. "Or does he merely think that that was a famous composer?"

"Both, probably," said Breeda, "and he thinks that Harvey is someone who invented sherry."

"And that angina is a double-barrelled name for a girl?"

"Yes, and take penicillin," said Breeda.

"You mean that emporium that specializes in writing materials?"

"The very same. Well, one day. . . ."

But what Breeda was about to vouchsafe will never be known, for at that moment Pimmie re-entered the room.

"Up yer get," she said to me. "Dr. Grubbins says yer to go to the Waterloo Hospital and have yer nose cauterized."

"Dear God," I said. "Just as I feared. A red-hot poker to be shoved up my right nostril."

"Don't be silly," said Pimmie, getting me my coat, "they'll use a cauterizing stick."

"A *stick*? A *flaming brand*? I was supposed to come here for peace and quiet."

"Yer can't have peace and quiet until we stop yer

nosebleed," said Pimmie practically. "Here, get this coat on. I'm coming wit yer. Doctor's instructions."

"And the only worthwhile instructions he's given since leaving medical school," I said warmly. "How are we to get there?"

"Taxi," said Pimmie succinctly. "It's waiting."

The driver, we soon discovered, was an Irishman. He was a tiny, carunculated man who looked like a walnut with legs.

"Where will yer be going?" he asked.

"Waterloo Hospital," said Pimmie clearly.

"Waterloo . . . Waterloo . . ." mused the driver. "And where would that be?"

"Westminster Bridge," said Pimmie.

"Of course it is, of course it is," said the driver, slapping his forehead. "I'll have you there in a couple of jiffs."

We bundled into the car and wrapped ourselves in a blanket, for the night was bitterly cold. We progressed some way in silence.

"And I was going to wash me hair tonight," said Pimmie suddenly and reproachfully.

"I'm very sorry," I said contritely.

"Ah, don't give it a thought," said Pimmie, adding somewhat mysteriously, "I can sit on it."

"Can you?" I asked, imagining that this was some up-to-date method of cleansing hair.

"Yes," said Pimmie with satisfaction. "It's that long. I was offered seventy pounds for it recently."

"But you wouldn't look half so attractive bald," I pointed out.

"That's what I thought," said Pimmie, and we relapsed into silence again.

The cab stopped at some traffic lights and the driver

craned round to examine his fares. The blue and white street lighting lent a weird pallor to my bloodstained face.

"Are you all right in the back there, now?" asked the driver anxiously. "It's an awful lot of blood yer dribbling about in the back there. You wouldn't want to stop for a lie down, would yer?"

I looked at the rain-lashed, freezing pavements.

"No, I don't think so, thank you," I said.

"Have yer tried sticking something up yer nose?" asked the driver, suddenly struck by this powerful thought.

I explained that my right nostril had had so much rammed up it that it closely resembled a municipal rubbish dump. At the hospital, I explained, they intended to cauterize.

"That's what they used to do in the old days, isn't it?" asked the driver with considerable interest.

"How do you mean?" I asked, puzzled.

"Well, they'd hang, draw, and cauterize yous, wouldn't they?"

"No, no. That was something quite different," I said, adding, "I hope."

We arrived at the hospital after driving up a ramp that had a notice saying (I could have sworn to this), "No Protestants," but which later proved to read, "No Pedestrians." I attributed this misreading to my close association with the Irish throughout the evening.

We bustled inside and found it free of drugged hippies, meth drinkers, and little boys with tin potties jammed on their heads. In fact, the out-patients was deserted except for the duty nurse. She ushered us into a sort of tabernacle and laid me tenderly on a species of operating table.

A Question of Degrees

"The doctor will be with you in a minute," she said with reverence in her voice, as though announcing the Second Coming. Presently, what appeared to be a fourteen-year-old boy clad in a white coat made his appearance.

"Good evening, sir. Good evening," he said heartily, rubbing his hands together, obviously practicing for Harley Street. "You have a nosebleed, I understand, sir."

Seeing that my beard and moustache were stiff with congealed blood and that blood was still dribbling from my right nostril and that my clothing was plentifully bespattered with gore, I did not feel that this was a particularly brilliant and perceptive diagnosis.

"Yes," I said.

"Well," said the doctor, producing two pairs of forceps, "we'll just have a look at the damage, shall we, sir?"

He spread the nostril as wide as a bushman's with one pair of forceps and with the other proceeded to pull out several feet of bloodstained bandage.

"Ah, yes," he said intelligently, peering into the gory cavity thus revealed, "you appear to have something more up there, sir."

"They pushed everything they could find up there," I said. "It wouldn't surprise me if you found a brace of staff nurses and a matron or two lolling about in the labyrinthine passages of my sinus."

The doctor laughed nervously and removed a slab of cotton wool from my nostril.

"Ah," he said, peering up the nostril with a small torch. "Yes, I see. I have found the bleeding spot. As a matter of fact, you have got one or two large veins up there, sir, which would be well worth keeping an eye on."

"Thank you," I said.

I wondered how you kept an eye on a vein that was lurking in the dimmer recesses of the nose.

"Now," said the doctor, "a little cocaine to, you know, kill it, as it were."

He seized something like a scent spray and squirted cocaine up my nose.

"That's it," he went on chattily. "Now, nurse, if I can have the cautery stick? That's it. Now, this won't hurt, sir."

Curiously enough, it did not hurt.

"That's it," said the doctor again, standing back with the air of a conjurer who has just successfully performed a particularly complicated trick.

"You mean that's all?" I asked in astonishment.

"Yes," said the doctor, peering up the nose with his torch, "that's all. It shouldn't give you any more trouble, sir."

"I really am most grateful," I said, vacating the operating table with alacrity.

Pimmie and I made our way out to where the taxi was waiting.

"My, that was quick," said the driver admiringly. "I quite thought yer'd be in there an hour or a couple."

"No, they made a very quick job of it," I said, taking deep, unrestrained, and joyful breaths through my nose.

The taxi rumbled down the ramp and into the street.

"Holy Mary, Mother of God!" said Pimmie suddenly and with considerable vehemence.

"What's the matter?" asked the driver and I in unison, startled.

"We've been to the wrong hospital," said Pimmie faintly.

"Wrong hospital? What do you mean?" I asked.

"Wrong hospital? No, that was the one you asked for," said the driver aggrievedly.

"It wasn't," said Pimmie. "It said Saint Thomas's on the side. We were supposed to go to the Waterloo."

"But it's by the bridge. You *said* by the bridge," the driver pointed out. "Look, *there's* the bridge."

He gave the impression that life was quite difficult enough without the added complication of somebody shifting all the London hospitals around.

"I don't care *where* it is," said Pimmie, "it's the wrong hospital. It's not the Waterloo."

"Does it matter?" I asked. "After all, they did the job."

"Yes, but I'd *alerted* the Waterloo," Pimmie explained. "The night staff were expecting us."

"Come to think of it," said the driver thoughtfully, "Waterloo does sound a little bit like Saint Thomas's, if you follow me, especially if yer driving a cab."

There did not seem to be a really adequate reply to this.

We returned to Abbotsford and while I sat drinking gallons of lukewarm tea, Pimmie went to phone the Waterloo hospital and explain the confusion.

"I told them it was your fault," she said triumphantly on her return. "I said you were a bit nutty and we put yer in a taxi and yer'd given the taxi driver the wrong hospital."

"Thanks very much," I said.

That night and the following day passed uneventfully except that another patient endeavored to sell me a fake Louis Quinze dining table in the reception hall and another one insisted on practicing Morse code on my door. However, these were minor irritations and my nose behaved beautifully.

When Pimmie came on night duty that evening she fixed me with a basilisk stare.

"Well," she inquired, "have yer had any more trouble with yer nose?"

"Not a thing," I said with pride, and the words were hardly out of my mouth when my nose started to bleed again.

"Dear God! Why d'yer have to wait until I come on duty?" inquired Pimmie. "Why can't yer give the day nurses a treat?"

"It's your beauty, Pimmie," I said. "It sends my blood pressure up and starts my nose bleeding."

"Whereabouts in Ireland did yer say yer came from?" inquired Pimmie, busy stuffing an adrenalin-soaked bandage up my nose.

"Gomorrah, on the borders of Sodom," I said promptly.

"I don't believe yer," said Pimmie, "although ye've got enough blarney for five ordinary Irishmen."

But her ministrations with the bandage were of no avail. The nose continued to drip like a tap with a faulty washer. Eventually Pimmie gave up exhausted and went to phone Dr. Grubbins for further instructions.

"Dr. Grubbins says yer to go to the Waterloo Hospital," she said on her return, "and he says will yer try and get the right hospital this time."

"Aren't you coming?" I asked.

"No," said Pimmie.

"But, why not?" I protested.

"I don't know the hell," said Pimmie. "But yer going in a staff car with a driver."

The staff car driver was determined to take his passenger's mind off his troubles.

"Nasty thing, nosebleeds," he said chattily. "We used

to get a lot of them when I played rugger, but I'm getting too old for that now."

"Too old for nosebleeds?" I inquired.

"No, no. For rugger, I mean," said the driver. "Do you play at all yourself, sir?"

"No," I said. "I dislike all organized ball games except one."

"And which one is that, sir?" asked the driver with interest.

It was obvious that he could hold forth in the same boring manner about any game that had ever been invented. He must be silenced at all costs.

"Sex," I said brutally, and we travelled the rest of the way in silence.

At the hospital a pleasant night sister led me into a ward which was almost deserted, except for an old man in a remote bed, coughing and trembling his way along the brink of the grave, and at a table some six feet away from and east of my bed a family group of father, mother, daughter, and son, playing Monopoly. I listened to their conversation in a desultory manner as I got ready for bed as instructed.

"Are you sure it won't 'urt, Mum?" asked the boy, shaking the dice vigorously.

"Corse it won't, dear," said the mother. "You 'erd what the doctor said."

"Corse it won't," echoed the father. "It's only your tonsils and your hadenoids. 'Tisn't as though it was a big job, like."

"Corse, it's only a small operation," said the mother. "You won't feel anything at all."

"I want to buy Picadilly," said the girl shrilly.

"You've seen 'em on the telly, 'aven't you?" asked the

father. "They don't feel a thing. Even when it's big things like taking the 'art out."

"'Enry!" said the mother quellingly.

"Picadilly, Picadilly. I want Picadilly," said the little girl.

"But it's *afterwards*," said the boy. "It's *afterwards*, when I come round, like. *Then* it'll 'urt, I expect."

"Na," said his father. "Na, corse it won't. They'll 'ave you under sedition."

"What's that?" asked the boy.

"Drugs and things, dear," said his mother soothingly. "'Onest, you won't feel a thing. Come on, it's your turn."

Poor little devil, I thought. Scared as hell, and the sight of me all covered with congealed blood can't possibly do his morale any good. Never mind, I'll have a few words with him afterwards when I'm cleaned up.

At that moment the nurse arrived.

"The doctor's coming up to do your nose now," she said, drawing the curtains round the bed.

"Ah," I said pleasedly. "Is he going to cauterize it again?"

"I don't expect so," said the nurse. "Dr. Veraswami likes plugging."

Plugging, I thought, what a beautiful word. It summed up the plumbers' art so succinctly. I plug, thou pluggest, he plugs, I thought. We pluggey, you pluggest, they plug. I stuff, thou stuffest, he stuffs. . . .

But my thoughts on the English verbs were interrupted by the arrival of Dr. Veraswami, who was a dark fawn color and surveyed the world through enormous pebble spectacles. His hands, I noticed with satisfaction, were as slender as a girl's, each long finger being very little thicker than the average cigarette. The sort of hands that are so delicate they remind you of butterflies.

Slim, elegant, fluttering, and incapable of hurt. A healer's hands. Dr. Veraswami examined my nose, giving tiny falsetto grunts to indicate alarm at what he found.

"Ve vill have to plug the nose," he said at last, smiling down at me.

"Help yourself," I said hospitably. "Anything to stop it bleeding."

"Nurse you vill kindly get the things," said the doctor, "then ve can begin."

The nurse trotted off and the doctor stood at the end of the bed and waited.

"Which part of India are you from?" I asked conversationally.

"I am not coming from India. I am from Ceylon," said the doctor.

Black mark, I thought; I must be careful.

"It's a beautiful country, Ceylon," I said heartily.

"Do you know it?" inquired the doctor.

"Well, not exactly. I once spent a week in Trincomalee. But I wouldn't call that *knowing* Ceylon," I said. "But I believe it's very beautiful."

The doctor, thus encouraged, went off like a travel poster.

"Very beautiful. On the coast ve have the coast with many palm trees, sandy beaches, and sea breezes. Plenty of things to shoot. Then ye have the foothills, banana plantations, and so forth. Very rich, very verdant. Plenty of things to shoot. Then there is the mountains. Very high, very green, many cool breezes. Views of the most stupendous imagination. Plenty of things to shoot."

"It sounds wonderful," I said uncertainly.

I was spared further eulogies on Ceylon by the reappearance of the nurse bearing the necessary accoutrements for the nose-plugging operation.

"Now, nurse," said the doctor busily, "vill you just hold the gentleman's head steady. That's it."

He seized on the end of what appeared to be a bandage some three miles long with the end of a pair of sharply pointed forceps with very long blades. Then he strapped a light to his head and advanced upon me. The nurse's grip on my skull tightened perceptibly. I wondered why. After all, Pimmie had plugged my nose with bandage and it had not hurt. The doctor plunged the forceps holding the bandage into my nostril and the pointed ends came to rest somewhere, it appeared, at the base of my skull, having penetrated my sinus, and left a searing trail of pain behind them. So severe was the pain that it paralysed my vocal cords so that I could not even utter a protest. The doctor removed the forceps and gathered up a foot or so of the bandage. This he plugged into the nostril and rammed it home with all the dedication of a duelist making sure that his pistol is primed. As he was packing the bandage home, his enthusiasm occasionally got the better of him and the pointed forceps would cut a groove in the delicate skin of the sinus. It now felt as though the nostril was being packed with red hot coals. Although my vocal cords had now returned to normal, I was prevented from voicing a protest for another reason. The Monopoly party had fallen silent and were listening avidly to the faint sounds that were coming from the curtain-shrouded bed. If, as my reason dictated, I uttered screams of pain, kicked Veraswami in the crotch, and then burst from behind the curtains trailing yards of bandage in a wild bid to obtain freedom, this could only undermine the morale of the small boy now nervously awaiting his own operation. I would just have to put up with it. The nurse, in order to hold my head steady, had it clasped in a vice-like grip. So firmly was she holding it that her thumbs made two circular bruises over my eyebrows which did not fade for some days.

Veraswami continued to pack foot after foot of bandage into the offending nostril, pecking away at his task with the eagerness of a blackbird worming on an early morning lawn. When we reached what appeared to be the half-way mark, I rather hoarsely asked for a brief cessation in hostilities.

"Is it hurting?" asked Veraswami with what could have been academic interest but sounded more like relish.

"Yes," I said.

The whole right-hand side of my skull, face, and neck throbbed and ached as though it had been pounded with a sledge hammer and I felt that an egg dropped into my sinus would fry to a turn.

"Ve have to be cruel to be kind," explained Veraswami, obviously delighted that his command over the English language had allowed him to use this well-worn maxim. The rest of the bandage (eleven feet of it, I discovered later) was packed in and then firmly wedged into place by Veraswami's thumbs, which had ceased to be ethereal and butterfly-like. I had read of tears spurting from people's eyes either from pain or grief and had always considered this to be poetic license. I now learned differently. Under the ministration of Veraswami's thumbs the tears of pain spurted from my screwed-up eyes like machine-gun bullets. Veraswami gave the bandage a final prod to make sure and then stood back with a satisfied smile.

"There," he said. "That should fix it."

I lifted my savagely aching head off the pillow and surveyed Veraswami.

"Has anyone ever suggested to you, doctor, that you give up trying to heal the sick and take up taxidermy?" I asked.

"No, no one," said Dr. Veraswami, puzzled.

I eased myself off the bed and started putting on my clothes.

"Well, I should try it," I said. "In taxidermy you get no complaints from your patients."

Veraswami had watched me dressing with increasing alarm.

"But, vere are you going?" he asked. "You can't leave. Not now. Supposing your nose started the bleeding again, I vould be left vith the can."

"Take your forceps to a quiet corner and sit on them," I advised tiredly. "I'm going back to Abbotsford."

I found a taxi and drove back in it, thinking evil thoughts about the medical profession in general and Dr. Veraswami in particular. I remembered that even in the 1920s if you took a short course in medicine in France, you were not allowed to practice medicine in France but your papers were marked "Suitable for the Orient." I wondered whether this was the Orient's revenge.

Then I remembered the story, probably apocryphal, about the Indian who wanted above all else to get his B.Sc. He sat exams year after year and failed. At last, in desperation, the authorities suggested that he give up trying to get a degree and turn his talents elsewhere. So he became an adviser on how to obtain the B.Sc., and to prove his worth he had cards printed which read, "Mr. Ram Sing, B.Sc. (failed)." Obviously, I thought, nursing my aching head, Veraswami (whose Christian name was probably Chipati) was what was known in the profession as Chipati Veraswami, M.D. (failed).

I arrived back at Abbotsford and Pimmie took a swift look at me.

"Did they fix it?" she asked.

"Don't touch me," I said. "They butchered me and I'm one gigantic exposed nerve ending. Offer me euthanasia and I'll be your friend for life."

"Into bed wit yer," said Pimmie. "I'll be back in a moment."

Tiredly, I removed my clothing and flopped into bed. Anything, even death, I thought, would be preferable to the pain I was now experiencing. I remembered, somewhat wryly, that I had come to Abbotsford for peace and quiet.

Pimmie entered the room with a hypodermic.

"Give me yer behind," she commanded. "Morphine. Doctor's orders."

She administered the drug deftly and then peered at my face with great earnestness. I was not a prepossessing sight. My right eye was swollen and half closed, my nostril spread wide like a boxer's by the preponderance of bandage, my beard and moustache an unlovely filigree of matted blood. She drew in her breath sharply and frowned.

"Sure and if I had them here I'd give them a bit of me mind," she said with sudden savagely.

"It's sweet of you to care," I said drowsily. "I didn't know you worried about me."

Pimmie drew herself up sharply.

"Worry about you?" she asked witheringly. "I'm not worried about you. It's all the extra work they've given me. That's what worries me. You go to sleep now and stop yer blarney."

She went to the door.

"I'll be back in a moment," she said, "and don't let me find you awake."

Chipati Veraswami, I thought, soothed on a cushion of morphia, M.D. (failed). Pimmie could teach him a thing or two. She passed.

❈ Ursula ❈

IN MY EARLY TWENTIES quite a number of personable young ladies drifted in and out of my life and none of them made a very deep impression upon me with the exception of Ursula Pendragon White. She popped in and out of my life for a number of years with monotonous regularity, like a cuckoo out of a clock, and of all the girl friends I had, I found that she was the only one who could arouse feeling in me that ranged from alarm and despondency to breathless admiration and sheer horror.

Ursula first came to my attention on the top of a Number 27 bus that was progressing in a stately fashion through the streets of Bournemouth, that most salubrious of seaside resorts, where I then lived. I occupied the back seat of the bus while Ursula and her escort occupied the front seat. It is possible that my attention would not have been attracted to her if it hadn't been for her voice which was melodious and as penetrating and all-pervading as the song of a roller canary. Looking around to find the source of these dulcet Rhodean accents I caught sight of Ursula's profile and was immediately riveted. She had dark, naturally curly hair, which she wore short in a sort of dusky halo round her head, and it framed a face that was both beautiful and remarkable. Her eyes were enormous and of that very deep blue, almost violet color, that forget-me-nots go in the sun, fringed with very dark, very long lashes, and set under very dark, permanently raised eyebrows. Her mouth was of the texture and quality that should never, under any circumstances, be used for eating kippers or frogs' legs or black pudding, and her teeth were very white and even. But it was her nose that was breath-taking; I had never seen a nose like it. It was long, but not too long, and combined three separate styles. It started off by being Grecian in the strict classical sense, but at the end the most extraordinary things happened to it. It suddenly tip-tilted like the nose of a very elegant pekingese, and then it was as though some-body had delicately sliced off the tip of the tilt to make it flat. Written down baldly like this it sounds most unattractive, but I can assure you the effect was enchant-ing. Young men took one look at Ursula's nose and fell deeply and blindly in love with it. It was a nose so charming and so unique that you could not wait to get on more intimate terms with it. So entranced was I by her nose that it was some moments before I came to and started eavesdropping on her conversation. It was then that I discovered another of Ursula's charms, and that was her grim, determined, unremitting battle with the English language. Where other people meekly speak their mother tongue in the way that it is taught to them, Ursula adopted a more militant and Boadicea-like approach. She seized the English language by the scruff of the neck, as it were, and shook it thoroughly, turned it inside out, and forced words and phrases to do her bidding, forced them to express things they were never meant to express.

Now she leant forward to her companion and said, apropos of something they had been discussing when I had got on the bus, "And Daddy says it's a half a dozen of one and a dozen of the other, but I don't think so. There's fire without smoke and *I* think somebody ought to tell her. Don't you?"

The young man, who looked like a dyspeptic bloodhound, seemed as confused at this statement as I was.

"Dunno," he said. "Ticklish situation, eh?"

"There's nothing funny about it, darling. It's serious."

"Some people," said the young man with the air of a Greek philosopher vouchsafing a pearl of wisdom, "some people never let their right hand know what their left hand is doing."

"My dear!" said Ursula, shocked, "I never let either of my hands know what I'm doing, but that's not the point. What I say is. . . . Ooooo! This is where we get off. Darling, hurry up."

I watched her as they threaded their way down the bus. She was tall, carelessly but elegantly dressed, with one of those willowy, coltish figures that turn young men's thoughts to lechery, and she had long and beautifully shaped legs. I watched her get down onto the pavement and then, still talking animatedly to her companion, disappear among the crowds of shoppers and holiday-makers.

I sighed. She was such a lovely girl that it seemed cruel of fate to have given me a tantalizing glimpse of her and then to whisk her out of my life. But I was wrong, for within three days Ursula had been whisked back into my life, where she remained, intermittently, for the next five years.

I had been invited to a friend's house to celebrate his birthday, and as I entered the drawing room I heard the clear, flute-like voice of the girl on the bus.

"I'm just a natural voyeur," she was saying earnestly

to a tall young man. "Travel is in my blood. Daddy says I'm the original rolling moss."

"Happy birthday," I said to my host. "And in return for this extremely expensive present I want you to introduce me to the girl with the extraordinary nose."

"What, Ursula?" he asked in surprise. "You don't want to meet *her*, do you?"

"It's my greatest ambition in life," I assured him.

"Well, on your own head be it," he said. "If she takes you up she'll drive you mad. The local asylum is already bursting with her various boy friends."

We moved across the room to the girl with the ravishing nose.

"Ursula," said my friend, trying to keep the surprise out of his voice, "here's somebody who wants to meet you. Gerry Durrell . . . Ursula Pendragon White."

Ursula turned and enveloped me in a blue stare of prickling intensity, and gave me a ravishing smile. Her nose, seen full-face, was even more enchanting than seen profile. I gazed at her and was lost.

"Hullo," she said. "You're the bug boy, aren't you?"

"I would prefer to be known as the elegant, handsome, witty, devil-may-care man-about-town," I said regretfully. "But if it is your wish that I be the bug boy, then the bug boy I shall be."

She gave a laugh that sounded like sleigh-bells.

"I'm sorry," she said. "That was rude of me. But you are the person who likes animals, aren't you?"

"Yes," I admitted.

"Then you're just the person I want to talk to. I've been arguing with Cedric for days about it. He's terribly stubborn, but I know I'm right. Dogs *can* have inhibitions, can't they?"

186

"Well . . ." I said judiciously, "if you beat them seven days a week. . . ."

"No, no, *no!*" said Ursula impatiently, as to a dim-witted child, "*inhibitions.* You know, they can see ghosts and tell when you're going to die, and all that sort of thing."

"Don't you mean premonitions?" I suggested tentatively.

"No, I don't," said Ursula sharply. "I mean what I say."

After we had discussed the noble qualities of dogs and their soothsaying prowess for some time, I cunningly steered the conversation on to music. There was a concert on at the Pavilion for which I had managed to acquire seats, and I thought that this would be a very dignified and cultural way of beginning my friendship with Ursula. Did she, I asked, like music?

"I simply *adore* it," she said, closing her eyes blissfully. "If music be the bowl of love, play on."

She opened her eyes and beamed at me.

"Don't you mean. . ." I began unguardedly.

From being warm and blurred as love-in-the-mist, Ursula's eyes suddenly became as sharp and angry as periwinkles under ice.

"Now don't *you* start telling me what I mean," she said mutinously. "All my boy friends do it and it makes me *wild.* They go on correcting and correcting me as though I was an . . . an exam paper or something."

"You didn't let me finish," I said blandly. "I was about to say, 'Don't you mean that your love of music is so great that you would accept with delight an invitation to a concert at the Pavilion tomorrow afternoon?'"

"Ooooo!" she exclaimed, her eyes glowing. "You haven't got tickets, have you?"

"It's the accepted way of getting into a concert," I pointed out.

"You are *clever*. I tried to get some last week and they were sold out. I'd *love* to come!"

As I left, feeling very pleased with myself, my host asked me how I had got on with Ursula.

"Wonderfully," I said, elated with my success. "I'm taking her out to lunch tomorrow and then to a concert."

"What?" exclaimed my host in horror.

"Jealousy will get you nowhere," I said. "You're a nice enough chap in your humble, uncouth way, but when it comes to attractive girls like Ursula you need a bit of charm, a bit of the old bubbling wit, a touch of the *je ne sais quoi*."

"I cannot do it," said my host. "In spite of your appalling arrogance. I cannot let *you*, a friend of mine, rush headlong into one of the blackest pits of hell without stretching out a hand to help save you."

"What are you talking about?" I asked, genuinely interested, for he seemed serious.

"Listen," he said earnestly, "be warned. The best thing would be for you to phone her up this evening and tell her you've got flu or rabies or something, but I know you won't do that. You're besotted. But for heaven's sake, take my advice. If you take her out to lunch, keep her away from the menu, unless somebody's just died and left you a couple of hundred pounds. She has an appetite like a particularly rapacious python, and no sense of money. As to the concert . . . well, don't you realize, my dear fellow, that the Pavilion authorities go pale and tremble at the mere mention of her name? That they have been trying for years to think of a legal way of banning her from attending concerts?"

"But she said she was very fond of music," I said uneasily.

"So she is, and it has a horrifying effect upon her. But not nearly as horrifying an effect as she has on music. I've seen the leader of the orchestra in tears, gulping sal volatile like a baby sucking its bottle, after a performance of *The Magic Flute*. And it's rumored, I think quite rightly, that the conductor's hair went white overnight after she'd attended a performance of Stravinsky's *Rite of Spring*. Don't you realize that when Eileen Joyce gave a recital here and Ursula attended she had such a detrimental effect upon that unfortunate pianist that she *forgot to change her dress* between pieces?"

"It . . . it could have been an oversight," I said.

"An oversight! An oversight? Tell me, have you ever known Eileen Joyce to run out of dresses?"

I must confess he had me there.

He propelled me with the gentleness of a kindly hangman to the front door.

"Don't forget," he said in a low voice, squeezing my arm with sympathy, "I'm your friend. If you need me, phone me. Any hour of the day or night. I'll be here."

And he shut the front door firmly in my face and left me to walk home, curiously disquieted.

But the following morning my spirits had revived. After all, I thought, Ursula was an exceptionally lovely girl and I was quite sure that anyone as attractive as that could not behave in the boorish manner that my friend had described. Probably he had tried to date her and she, being wise as well as beautiful, had given him the brush-off. Comforting myself with this thought, I dressed with unusual care and went down to the rail-way station to meet her. She had explained that, living out in Lyndhurst in the New Forest, she had to come into Bournemouth by train because "Daddy always uses the Rolls when I want it." On the platform I awaited the arrival of the train anxiously.

Whilst I was rearranging my tie for the twentieth time I was accosted by an elderly lady, a pillar of the local church, who was, unaccountably, a friend of my mother's. I stood, shifting nervously from one foot to the other, wishing the old harridan would go away, for when meeting a new girl friend for the first time, the last thing one wants is a sanctimonious and critical audience. But she clung like a leech and was still telling me about her latest jumble sale when the train dragged itself, chugging and grimy, into the station. I was giving scant attention to her story of what the vicar said. I was too busy looking at the opening carriage doors and trying to spot Ursula.

"And the vicar said, 'I, myself, Mrs. Darlinghurst, will tell the bishop about your selfless dedication to the organ fund.' He has no need to say it, of course, but I thought it was most Christian of him, don't you?"

"Oh, yes . . . yes. . . . Most, er, perceptive of him."

"That's what I thought. So I said to him, 'Vicar,' I said, 'I'm only a humble widow. . . .'"

What other secrets of her private life she had vouchsafed to the vicar I was never to learn, because from behind me came an earsplitting scream of recognition.

"Darling! *Darling*, I'm here," came Ursula's voice.

I turned round, and only just in time, for Ursula flung herself into my arms and fastened her mouth on mine with the avidity of a starving bumble-bee sighting the first clover flower of the season. When I finally managed to extricate myself from Ursula's octopus-like embrace I looked round for Mrs. Darlinghurst, only to find her retreating along the platform, backwards, with a look on her face of one who, having led a sheltered life, suddenly finds himself confronted with the more unsavory aspects of a Roman orgy. I smiled feebly at her, waved goodbye, and then, taking Ursula firmly by the arm, steered her out of the station while endeavoring to remove what felt like several pounds of lipstick from my mouth.

Ursula was dressed in a very smart blue outfit that highlighted her unfairly enormous eyes, and she wore elegant white lace gloves. Over her arm she carried a curious basket like a miniature hamper with a large handle, which presumably contained sufficient cosmetics to withstand a siege of several years.

"Darling," she said, peering raptly into my face, "I am going to enjoy this. Such a lovely day! Lunch alone with you, and then the concert. . . . Uhhmmm! *Paradise!*"

A number of men in the ticket hall, on hearing her invest the word "paradise" with a sort of moaning lechery that had to be heard to be believed, looked at me enviously, and I began to feel better.

"I've booked a table. . ." I began.

"Darling," interrupted Ursula, "I simply *must* go to the loo. There wasn't one on the train. Buy me a newspaper so I can go."

Several people stopped and stared.

"Hush!" I said hurriedly. "Not so loud. What do you want a newspaper for? They have paper in the loos."

"Yes, but it's so *thin*, darling. I like a nice thick layer on the seat," she explained, in a clear voice that carried like a chime of bells on a frosty night.

"On the seat?" I asked.

"Yes. I *never* sit on the seat," she said. "Because I knew a girl once who sat on a loo seat and got acme."

"Don't you mean acne?" I asked, confused.

"No, *no!*" she said impatiently. "Acme. You come out all over in the most hideous red spots. Do hurry and buy me a newspaper, darling. I'm simply *dying*."

So I bought her a paper and watched her disappear into the ladies, flourishing it as a deterrent to germs, and I wondered if any one of her numerous boy friends had ever described her as the acne of perfection.

She emerged, several minutes later, smiling and apparently germfree, and I bundled her into a taxi and drove her to the restaurant. When we got there and had established ourselves the waiter unfurled two enormous menus in front of us. Remembering my friend's advice I removed the menu deftly from Ursula's hands.

"I'll choose for you," I said. "I'm a gourmet."

"Are you really?" said Ursula. "But you're not Indian, are you?"

"What has that got to do with it?" I inquired.

"Well, I thought they came from India," she said.

"What? Gourmets?" I asked, puzzled.

"Yes," she said. "Aren't they those people that spend all their time looking at their tummy?"

"No, no. You're thinking of something quite different," I said. "Anyway, be quiet and let me order."

I ordered a modest but substantial lunch and a bottle of wine to go with it. Ursula chattered on endlessly. She had an enormous variety of friends, all of whom she expected you to know, and whose every concern was of interest to her. From the stories that she told, it was obvious that she spent the greater part of her life trying to reorganize the lives of her friends, whether they wanted her to or not. She babbled on like a brook and I listened entranced.

"I'm very worried about Toby," she confided to me

over the prawn cocktail. "I'm very worried about him indeed. I think he's got a secret passion for someone and it's just eating him away. But Daddy doesn't agree with me. Daddy says he's well on the way to being an incoherent."

"An incoherent?"

"Yes. You know, he drinks too much."

So rich is the English language, I reflected, that this word could, in fact, with all fairness, be used to describe a drunk.

"He ought to join Incoherents Anonymous," I said without thinking.

"What are they?" asked Ursula, wide-eyed.

"Well, they're a sort of secret society of . . . of . . . um . . . incoherents, who try and help each other to . . . well, to give it up and become . . . um . . . become. . ."

"Become coherents!" said Ursula with a squeak of delight.

I must confess this end result had escaped me.

Later on, over her filet mignon, she leant forward and fixed me with her blue, intense stare.

"Do you know about Susan?" she whispered. Her whisper was more clearly audible than her normal voice.

"Er . . . no," I confessed.

"Well, she became pregnant. She was going to have an *illiterate baby*."

I pondered this news. "With modern methods of education. . ." I began.

"Don't be silly! She didn't use *anything*," whispered Ursula. "That's what's so *stupid*. And her father, naturally, said he wasn't going to have a lot of illiterates darkening *his* hearth."

"Naturally," I said. "It would turn it into a sort of Do-the-girls Hall."

"Exactly!" she said. "So her father said she must have an ablution."

"To wash away sin?" I inquired.

"No, silly! To get rid of the baby."

"And did she have it?" I asked.

"Yes. He sent her up to London. It cost an awful lot of money and the poor dear came back looking terrible. I do think her father was unfair."

By this time most of the other tables in the restaurant were listening to our conversation with bated breath.

Over coffee Ursula was telling me a long and very involved story about some friend of hers who was in dire distress, whom she had wanted to help. I hadn't listened with any great attention until she suddenly said, "Well, I couldn't do anything about it *then*, because Mummy was in bed with a cold and Daddy wanted me to cook him an early lunch because he was taking the bull to the vet to have him castigated. And so. . . ."

"Your father was doing *what?*" I asked.

"Taking the bull to the vet to have him castigated. He was getting terribly fierce and dangerous."

How, I wondered, enraptured by the thought, did one castigate a fierce and dangerous bull? But I was too wise to ask Ursula.

"Look, hurry up and finish your coffee," I said. "Otherwise we'll be late for the concert."

"Oooo, yes," she said. "We mustn't be late."

She gulped down her coffee and I paid the bill and ushered her out of the restaurant. We walked through what are laughingly called the Pleasure Gardens of Bournemouth among the faded rhododendrons and the paddling pool, and came eventually to the Pavilion.

As we made our way to our seats, Ursula insisted on taking her miniature hamper with her.

"Why don't you leave it in the cloakroom?" I asked, for it was a fairly bulky object.

"I don't trust cloakrooms," said Ursula darkly. "They do strange things in cloakrooms."

In order to save embarrassment I didn't inquire what strange things they did in cloakrooms, and we got into our seats and wedged the hamper between our legs.

Gradually the Pavilion filled with the normal crowd of earnest music lovers. And when the leader of the orchestra appeared, Ursula joined in the clapping with great vigor and then she leaned across to me and said, "I think he's such a handsome conductor, don't you?"

I didn't feel that at that moment I should correct her. Presently the conductor came on and again Ursula threw herself into the applause with great enthusiasm and settled back with a deep sigh. She glanced at me and gave me a ravishing smile.

"I *am* going to enjoy this, darling," she said.

The concert was a hotchpotch of Mozart, a composer I am very fond of. I soon discovered what my friends had meant about Ursula's distressing effect upon music. Should there be the slightest pause for one brief second in the music, Ursula's hands were up and clapping. Soon, after people had been hissing and shushing us, I became quite adroit at catching her hands as they came up to clap in the middle of a piece. Each time she would turn anguished eyes on me and say, "Darling, I'm *sorry*. I thought he'd finished."

It was, I think, after the fourth piece that I felt the basket move. At first I thought I was mistaken but I pressed my leg against it and, sure enough, it was vibrating. I looked at Ursula, who had her eyes closed and was waving her forefinger in the air in time to the music.

"Ursula?" I whispered.

"Yes, darling," she said, without opening her eyes.

"What have you got in your basket?" I asked.

She opened her eyes, startled, and looked at me.

"What do you mean?" she said defensively.

"There is something moving in your basket," I said.

"Hush!" came a chorus of angry voices around us.

"But it can't be," she said, "unless the pill's worn off."

"*What* have you got in your basket?" I asked.

"Oh, it's nothing. It's just a present for somebody," she said.

She leant down and fumbled at the lid, raised it, and then lifted out of it a minute, snow-white pekingese with enormous black eyes.

To say I was shocked would be putting it mildly. After all, the concert-goers in Bournemouth took their music very seriously, and the last thing that they wanted or, indeed, would have allowed, was a dog in the sacred precincts of the Pavilion.

"Oh, damn!" said Ursula, looking at the pekingese's rather charming little snub nose. "The pill's worn off."

"Look, put him back in the basket!" I hissed.

"Hush!" said everybody around us.

Ursula bent down to put the puppy back into the basket and he yawned voluptuously into her face and then gave a sudden and unexpected wiggle. She dropped him.

"Oooo!" she squeaked. "I dropped him! I dropped him!"

"Shut up!" I said.

"Hush!" said everyone around us.

I reached down to try and find the puppy, but, obviously exhilarated by the fact that he had been released from his prison, he had trotted down the row through the forest of legs.

"What are we going to *do?*" said Ursula.

"Look, just shut up! Shut up and leave it to me," I said.

"Hush!" said everybody around us.

We hushed for a minute while I thought frantically. How could I possibly find a pekingese puppy amongst all those seats and legs without disrupting the entire concert?

"We'll have to leave it," I said. "I'll look for him after everybody's gone, after the concert."

"You can't!" said Ursula. "You simply can't leave him, poor little thing. He might get trodden on and hurt."

"Well, how do you expect me to find him?" I asked.

"Hush!" said everybody around us.

"He's got all tangled up in the seats and the legs and things," I said.

"But darling, you *must* find him. He'll get terribly, terribly lonely," she said.

There must have been all of seven hundred people in the hall.

"All right," I said. "I'll pretend I'm going to the loo."

"What a good idea," said Ursula, beaming. "I think he went down that way."

I got to my feet and ran the gauntlet of outraged faces and mumbled profanity as I worked my way down the row and out into the aisle. There, I saw just ahead of me the pekingese puppy, squatting down as boy puppies do before they've learnt to cock their leg, decorating the red carpet with a little sign of his own. I went forward cautiously and grabbed at him. I caught him, but as I lifted him up he uttered a loud and piercing scream that was clearly audible even above the rather exuberant piece of music that the orchestra was playing. There was a great rustle as people turned round indignantly to look in my direction. The puppy continued his screams. I stuffed him unceremoniously under my coat, and, almost at a run, I left the concert hall.

I went to the cloakroom, where, fortunately, I knew the girl in charge.

"Hullo," she said. "You leaving already? Don't you like the concert?"

"No ... it's ... it's a question of force of circumstances," I said. I pulled the puppy out from my jacket and held it up in front of her.

"Would you look after this for me?" I asked.

"Oh, isn't he sweet!" she said. "But you didn't have him in there, did you? Dogs are not allowed you know."

"Yes, I know," I said. "He just got in by mistake. He belongs to a friend of mine. Would you look after him till after the concert?"

"Of *course* I will," she said. "Isn't he sweet?"

"He's not terribly sweet when he's in a concert hall," I said.

I handed the puppy over to her tender care and went back and stood quietly in the shadows until the orchestra had finished the piece that they were playing. Then I made my way back to Ursula.

"Have you got him, darling?" she asked.

"No, I haven't," I said. "I put him in charge of the cloakroom attendant. She's a friend of mine."

"Are you sure he'll be all right?" she asked, obviously with dark thoughts about what they did in cloakrooms to pekingese puppies.

"He'll be perfectly all right," I said. "He'll be loved and cherished until after the concert. I can't think what induced you to bring a dog to a concert."

"But, darling," she said, "I meant him as a present for a friend of mine. I ... I meant to tell you only you

198

talked so much that I couldn't get a word in edgeways. I want to take him after the concert."

"Well, don't, for heaven's sake, do it again," I said. "The Pavilion is not a place for dogs. Now let's relax and try and enjoy the rest of the concert, shall we?"

"Of course, darling," she said.

When the concert was over and Ursula had, as she put it, clapped herself hoarse, we extricated the puppy from the cloakroom and put it back in its basket and made our way out through the throngs of music lovers avidly discussing the prowess of the Bournemouth Symphony Orchestra.

"Darling, I *did* enjoy that," said Ursula. "It's all those archipelagos. They go running up my spine. There's nothing like Beethoven, is there?" she asked loudly and clearly, hanging on my arm like a fragile maiden aunt, gazing earnestly into my eyes, and clasping in one hand the programme, which had embossed in large letters on the front, "A Concert of Mozart."

"Absolutely nothing," I agreed. "Now, what about this puppy?"

"Well," she said, "I want to take him to a friend of mine who lives on the outskirts of Poole. Her name is Mrs. Golightly."

"I'm not at all surprised," I said. "But why do you want to take the puppy to Mrs. Golightly?"

"She needs it," said Ursula. "She needs it desperately. You see, she's just lost her own Bow-wow."

"She's lost her what?" I asked.

"Her Bow-wow," said Ursula.

"You mean her dog?" I asked.

"Yes," said Ursula. "That's what he was called— Bow-wow."

"And so she needs another one?" I said.

"Of course," said Ursula. "She doesn't *want* one, but she needs one."

"Are you, um, giving her this puppy because you think she needs one?" I inquired.

"But of course! Anyone with half an eye could see she needs one," said Ursula.

"It strikes me," I said, "that you spend most of your time interfering in your friends' affairs when they don't really want it."

"Of course they want it," said Ursula earnestly. "They want it but they don't *realize* that they want it."

I gave up.

"All right," I said. "Let's go to Poole."

So we went. When we got to Poole, Ursula dived immediately into the back streets and eventually ended up at one of those tiny little houses, two up and two down, that stare frostily at each other across streets. This one had a highly polished brass door-knob and I noticed that the step was a beautiful white as evidence of hard scrubbing on someone's part. Ursula banged vigorously with the knocker and presently the door was opened by a tiny, grey, frail old lady.

"Why, Ursula!" she said. "Miss Ursula, it's you!"

"Emma, darling!" said Ursula and enveloped this fragile wisp of a person in a vast embrace.

"We've come to visit you," she said, unnecessarily. "This is Gerry."

"Oh, do . . . do come in," said the little old lady, "but I do wish you'd let me know. I'm all untidy and the house is in such a mess."

She ushered us into a living room full of the most ugly furniture I have ever seen in my life, that glowed with love and polish. It spoke of the most impeccable bad taste. It was a room which had been cherished as things are cherished in a museum. Nothing was out of place; everything glittered and gleamed and the air smelt faintly of furniture polish and antiseptic. Carefully arranged on the upright piano, which didn't look as though it had ever been used, were a series of photographs; two of them were portraits of a heavily moustached gentleman standing rather rigidly, and the rest were of a rather fluffy mongrel in various attitudes. Most of them were blurred and out of focus, but it was quite obvious that the moustached gentleman took second place to the dog. This, I suspected, must have been Bow-wow.

"Do sit down. Do sit down," said the little old lady. "I must make you a cup of tea. I've got some cake. What a merciful thing, I made a cake only the other day. You will have a slice of cake and a cup of tea?"

My one desire at the precise moment was for several very large pints of beer, but I said that I would be delighted with tea.

Over tea and a slice of sponge cake that was as light and frothy as a pound of lead, Ursula chattered on. It was obvious that Emma Golightly had, at some time, been somebody in her father's household for whom she quite obviously had a great affection. It was extraordinary to watch the effect of Ursula's exuberance on Emma. When she opened the door to us, her face had been grey and gaunt and now it was flushed and smiling and she was obviously injected with some of Ursula's enthusiasm.

"Yes, yes!" she kept saying, "and do you remember the time. . . ."

"But of course!" Ursula said. "And then do you remember that other time when. . . ." And so it went on interminably.

But it was as though this rather fragile little old lady had been given a transfusion. I almost expected to look at Ursula and find her drained completely of blood.

Eventually, with masterly adroitness, Ursula steered the subject on to Bow-wow.

"Er, Gerry doesn't know about Bow-wow," she said, looking at Emma commiseratingly. "You tell him."

Emma's eyes filled with tears.

"He was a wonderful dog," she said. "A wonderful dog. Really, you know, he could almost speak . . . almost speak, he really could, And then, one day, I let him out and some bloke in a car came down here and knocked him over. Didn't even stop . . . he didn't even stop. I took him to the vet . . . he was all covered with blood. I took him to the vet and I said . . . I'll pay anything, anything to keep him alive. 'Cos, you see, after my husband died, he was all I had. And he was a lovely dog, he really was. You would have loved him if you'd known him. And he was all covered with blood and he didn't seem to be suffering much, but they said there was nothing they could do. They said the kindest thing would be to put him out of his misery. Well, now, he'd been my companion ever since my husband died. For . . . for years I'd . . . I'd had him. . . . For nearly twelve years. And so you can imagine it was a bit of a shock to me. So as they said it was the only thing to do, I said, 'Well, all right, well – go ahead and do it.' And so they . . . they put him down."

She paused for a moment and blew her nose vigorously.

"It must have been a great shock to you," I said.

"Oh, it was. It was a tremendous shock. It was like taking away part of my life, because, as I said to you, ever since my husband died he'd really been my only companion."

I wasn't quite sure how to continue this conversation, because it was quite obvious that if Emma went on talking about Bow-wow she would break down and I didn't know how we could cope with that situation. But at that moment Ursula unveiled her guns.

"*Darling* Emma," she said, "it's *because* of the way you treated Bow-wow . . . the way that you looked after him and gave him such a happy life . . . it's for that reason that I want to . . . I want to ask you a *very great favor*. Now please say no, but I do wish that you'd consider it."

"A favor, Miss Ursula?" said Emma. "Of course I'll do you a favor. What do you want?"

"Well," said Ursula, prevaricating like mad, "this friend of mine has got this puppy and unfortunately, owing to illness in the family – his wife is desperately, *desperately* ill – he can't give it the attention that it really deserves, and so – just for a week or so – he wants somebody to look after it. Somebody who'll love it and give it the affection it needs. And immediately I thought of you."

"Oh," said Emma, "a puppy? Well, I . . . I don't know. I mean, after Bow-wow . . . you know, you don't seem to want another dog, somehow."

"But this is only a *puppy*," said Ursula, her eyes brimming. "Only a tiny, *tiny* little puppy. And it's only for a week or so. And I'm sure that you could look after it so *marvelously*."

"Well, I don't know, Miss Ursula," said Emma, "I . . . I wouldn't like to have another dog."

"But I'm not asking you to *have* it," said Ursula. "I'm just asking you to look after it for this poor man whose wife is terribly, *terribly* ill. He's torn between his wife and his dog."

"Ah," said Emma. "Just as I was when Bill was ill.

I remember it now. I sometimes didn't know whether to take Bow-wow out for a walk or stay with Bill, he was that sick. Well, what sort of a dog is it, Miss Ursula?"

"I'll show you," said Ursula. She bent down and opened the basket. The pekingese was lying curled up, exhausted by his cultural afternoon at the Pavilion, sound asleep. She picked him up unceremoniously by the scruff of his neck and held him up before Emma's startled eyes.

"Look at him," said Ursula. "*Poor little thing.*"

"Oh," said Emma, "Oh, poor little thing." She echoed Ursula unconsciously.

Ursula attempted to cradle the puppy in her arms and he gave her, to my satisfaction, a very sharp bite on the forefinger.

"*Look* at him," she said, her voice quivering, as he struggled in her arms. "A poor little dumb animal that doesn't really know whether he's coming or going. He's been wrenched away from the family life that he is used to. Surely you will take pity on him, Emma?"

I began to feel that the whole scene was beginning to take on the aspect of something out of *Jane Eyre*, but I was so fascinated by Ursula's technique that I let her go on.

"This tiny waif," she said, extricating her finger with difficulty from his champing jaws, "this tiny waif wants only a little bit of companionship, a little bit of help in his moment of strife. . . . As, indeed, does my friend."

"Well, I'll give you the fact that he's very, very nice," said Emma, obviously moved.

"Oh, he is," said Ursula, clamping her hand firmly over his mouth so that he couldn't bite her again. "He's absolutely charming, and I believe I'm not sure, but I believe he's house-trained. . . . Just for a week, dear Emma. Can't you possibly see your way to . . . to . . . to putting him up, as it were, as though he was a paying guest or something like that?"

"Well, I wouldn't do it for everybody," said Emma, her eyes fastened, mesmerized, on the wriggling fat-tummied, pink-tummied puppy with his great load of white fur and his great bulbous black eyes. "But seeing as he seems a nice little dog, and as it's you that's asking . . . I'm . . . I'm willing to have him for a week."

"Darling," said Ursula. "Bless you."

She whipped the puppy hastily back into his hamper because he was getting out of control. Then she rushed across and threw her arms round Emma and kissed her on both cheeks.

"I always knew," she said, peering into Emma's face with her brilliant blue searchlight gaze that I knew could have such devastating effect, "I knew that you, of *all* people, would not turn away from a tiny little puppy like this in his hour of need."

The curious thing was that she said it with such conviction that I almost got out my handkerchief and sobbed.

So eventually, refusing the offer of another cup of tea and another slice of indigestible cake, we left. As we walked down the road towards the station Ursula wrapped her arm round me and clutched me tight.

"Thank you *so* much, darling," she said. "You were a great help."

"What do you mean, a great help?" I said. "I didn't do anything."

"No, but you were there. Sort of . . . a sort of a force, a presence, you know?"

"Tell me," I said, interested, "why you want to inflict this poor woman with that vindictive little puppy when she obviously doesn't require one?"

"Oh, but you don't know about Emma," said Ursula. Which was quite true because I didn't.

"Tell me," I said.

"Well," she began. "First of all, her husband got ill and then they got Bow-wow and then her attention was divided between the husband and Bow-wow, and then the husband died and she channelled all her recuperance, or whatever you call it, into Bow-wow. And then Bow-wow got knocked down and since then she's been going steadily downhill. My dear, you could *see* it. Every time I came to visit her I could see that she was getting more and more sort of, well . . . you know, old and haggish."

"And how do you think the puppy is going to help her?" I inquired.

"Of course it's going to help her. It's the most savage puppy of the litter. It's bound to bite the postman or the greengrocer or somebody who delivers something, and it's got very long hair for a peke and it's going to shed that all over the place, and it's not house-trained so it's going to pee and poo all over the place, dear."

"Just a minute," I said, interrupting, "do you think this is a very wise gift to give a fragile old lady who's just lost her favorite Bow-wow?"

"But my dear, it's the *only* gift," said Ursula. She stopped, conveniently under a street lamp, and her eyes gazed up at me.

"Bow-wow used to be exactly the same. He left hair all over the place, and if she didn't let him out he'd pee in the hall, and she'd complain for days. . . . Gives her something to do. Well, since her husband died and Bow-wow died she's got nothing to do at all and she was just going into a sort of . . . a sort of grey *decline*. Now, with this new puppy, he'll bite her and he'll bite everyone else. They'll probably have court cases and he'll put his hair all over the place and he'll pee on the carpet and she'll be as delighted as anything."

I gazed at Ursula and for the first time I saw her for what she was.

"Do you know," I said, putting my arms round her and kissing her, "I think you're rather nice."

"It's not a question of niceness," said Ursula, disrobing herself on me, as it were. "It's not a question of niceness. She's just a pleasant old lady and I want her to have fun while she's still alive. That puppy will give her tremendous fun."

"But you know, I would never have thought of that," I said.

"Of *course* you would, darling," she said, giving me a brilliant smile. "You're so clever."

"Sometimes," I said as I took her arm and walked her down the street, "sometimes I begin to wonder whether I am."

The next few months had many halcyon days for me. Ursula possessed a sort of ignorant purity that commanded respect. I very soon found that in order to avoid embarrassment it was better to take her out into the countryside rather than confine her to a restaurant or theatre. At least in the countryside the cuckoos and larks and hedgehogs accepted her for what she was, a very natural and nice person. Take her into the confines of Bournemouth society and she dropped bricks at the rate of an unskilled navvy helping on a working site.

However, even introducing Ursula to the wilds was not without its hazards. I showed her a tiny strip of woodland that I'd discovered which had, at that time, more birds' nests per square inch than any other place I knew. Ursula got wildly excited and peered into nests brim-full of fat, open-mouthed baby birds or clutches of blue and brown eggs, and ooo'd over them delightedly. Nothing would content her but that I had to visit the place every day and phone her a long report on the progress of the various nests. A few weeks later I took her down to the place again and we discovered, to our horror, that it had been found, presumably by a group of schoolboys, and they had gone systematically through the whole of the woodland and destroyed every nest. The baby birds were lying dead on the ground and the eggs had all been taken. Ursula's anguish was intense. She sobbed uncontrollably with a mixture of rage and grief and it was a long time before I could comfort her.

She was still racked with occasional shuddering sobs when I ushered her into the spit and sawdust Bar of the Square and Compass, one of my favorite pubs in that region. Here, in this tiny bar, all the old men of the district would gather every evening, great brown lumbering shire horses of men, their faces as wrinkled as walnuts, their drooping moustaches as crisp and white as summer grass with frost on it. They were wonderful old men and I thought to meet them would take Ursula's mind off the ravaged nests. I was also interested to see what sort of reaction her presence would create.

To begin with, they sat stiff, silent, and suspicious, their hands carefully guarding their tankards, staring at us without expression. They knew me but now I had introduced an alien body into their tiny, smoke-blurred bar and, moreover, a very attractive and feminine body. This was heresy. The unwritten law was that no woman entered that bar. But Ursula was completely unaware of this or, if not unaware, undaunted by it. She powdered her nose, gulped down a very large gin in record time, and turned her brilliant melting blue eyes on the old men. Within a few minutes she had them relaxed and occasionally, half guiltily, chuckling with her. Then she spied the black board in the corner.

"Oooh!" she squeaked delightedly, "tiddleywinks!"

The old men exchanged looks of horror. Then they all looked at the oldest member of the group, an eighty-four-year-old patriarch who was, I knew, the local champion of this much beloved game.

"No, Miss," he said firmly, "that's shove ha'penny."

"Do teach me to play it," said Ursula, gazing at him so adoringly that his brown face went the color of an overripe tomato.

"Yes, go on, George, teach the Miss," the other old men chorused, delighted that George was coloring and shuffling like a schoolboy.

Reluctantly, he lumbered to his feet and he and Ursula moved over to the table where the shove ha'penny board lay in state.

As I watched him teaching her I realized, not for the first time, the deviousness of women in general and of Ursula in particular. It was perfectly obvious that she not only knew how to play shove ha'penny but probably could have beaten George at it. But her fumbling attempts to learn from him and the sight of him patting her shoulder with his enormous caruncled hand as gently as though he were patting a puppy were a delight to watch. Ursula lost gracefully to him and then insisted on buying drinks all round – for which I had to pay since she had no money.

By now, the old men, flushed and enthusiastic, were practically coming to blows over who should play her next. Ursula, armed with her indispensable evening newspaper, disappeared briefly into the ladies before coming back to challenge all comers.

George, wiping the froth off his magnificent moustache, lowered himself onto the oak trestle beside me and accepted a cigarette.

"A fine young woman, sir," he said, "a very fine young woman, even though she's a foreigner."

The curious thing is that he did not use the term foreigner in the way that most villagers in England would use it to describe somebody who had not actually been born in the village. He was firmly convinced by Ursula's particular brand of English that she must indeed come from the Continent or some savage place like that. I did not disillusion him.

I had known Ursula for about a year when one day she phoned me and dropped a bombshell.

"Gerry!" The voice was so penetrating that I had to hold the receiver away from my ear. It could only be Ursula.

"Yes," I said resignedly.

"Darling, it's *me*, Ursula."

"I never would have guessed it," I said. "You're so much quieter, so much more dulcet. That soft voice, like the cooing of a sucking dove. . . ."

"Don't be *silly*, darling. I phoned you up because I've got the most *wonderful* news and I wanted *you* to be the first to know," she said breathlessly.

What now, I wondered? Which one of her numerous friends had achieved some awful success due to her Machiavellian plottings?

"Tell me all," I said, resigning myself to at least half an hour of telephone conversation.

"Darling, I'm *engaged*," said Ursula.

I confess that my heart felt a sudden pang and a loneliness spread over me. It was not that I was in love with Ursula; it was not that I wanted to marry her – God forbid! – but suddenly I realized that I was being deprived of a charming companion. I was being deprived of somebody who could always lighten my gloom, and somebody who had given me so many hours of pleasure. And now she was engaged, doubtless to some hulking idiot, and all this, our lovely friendship, would change.

"Darling?" said Ursula. "Darling? Are you still there?"

"Yes," I said. "I'm still here."

"But, darling, you sound so glum. Is anything the matter? I thought you'd be *pleased!*" Her voice sounded plaintive, uncertain.

"I am pleased," I said, trying to cast away selfishness, trying to cast away the remembrance of Ursula telling me of a friend who'd gone to Venice and who'd had a gondolier every night. "Really, my love, I'm as pleased as punch. Who is the unlucky man?"

"It's Toby," she said. "You know Toby."

"But I thought he was an incoherent?" I said.

"No, no, silly. Not that Toby, a completely *different* one."

"I'm glad of that. I thought that if he was an incoherent he would have had difficulty in proposing."

"Darling, you don't sound a bit like *you*," she said, her voice worried and subdued. "Are you angry with me for getting engaged?"

"Not at all," I said acidly. "I'm delighted to know that you've found somebody who can stop you talking long enough to propose. I never could."

"Ooooo!" said Ursula. "You're jealous! Darling, how

wonderful! I never knew you wanted to propose to me. When was it?"

"Frequently," I said, tersely, "but fortunately I managed to stamp the desire underfoot."

"Oh, darling, I *am* sorry. Are you going to go all silent and withdrawn and morass?"

"I've not the slightest intention of turning myself into a bog for your benefit," I said with some asperity.

"Oh, darling, don't be so *silly*. I thought you'd be *pleased*. As a matter of fact I was hoping we could meet. . . ." Her voice trailed away.

What a cad I was being, I reflected. What a monstrous, inhuman cad. Here was the girl virtually asking me to set the seal on her nuptials and here was I behaving like a fifteen-year-old. I was contrite.

"Of course we can meet, my sweet," I said. "I'm sorry I was rude. It's just that I can't get used to the idea of you being engaged. Where do you want to meet?"

"Oh, darling, *that's* better. Why don't we dance away the evening? Let's go to the Tropicana. . . . *Do* let's, darling!"

Dance away the evening until ten o'clock, I thought to myself. The Tropicana was a particularly revolting nightclub of the sort that blossom suddenly like puffballs and have their brief moment of contributing to human misery and then mercifully disappear into obscurity. Of all the places she could have suggested Ursula could not have picked one that I disliked more.

"Right," I said with enthusiasm, "but can we have dinner first?"

"Oh darling, *yes*. Where?"

"How about the Grill room? I'll book a table."

"*Daarling!*" breathed Ursula. "The *first* place we had lunch together. Darling, you *are* romantic."

"Not particularly. It's just the only place that serves good food," I said austerely.

"Darling, I *love* you ... even if you *are* oppressive. Lovely food, and then dancing. Oh, I'll meet you at the Grill at eight, darling, I can't tell you how pleased I am that you're pleased. I *love* you and *love* you for ever."

I put the phone back and realized what I'd lost.

I realized what I'd lost even more when I met her, for she brought her fiancé with her. He was a handsome young man, quite obviously besotted by Ursula, with a very limited vocabulary. But he seemed nice enough. The Grill room, as I had rather suspected, was packed and so the three of us had to sit uncomfortably at a table designed for two. Toby didn't have very much to say for himself but that scarcely mattered as Ursula talked quite enough for two of them. When we'd finished dinner we went on to the Tropicana where the band was blaring. Here, Toby and I solemnly took it in turns to propel Ursula, chattering madly, round and round the floor. It was a thoroughly miserable evening, from my point of view. After that, I didn't see Ursula for a long time. I heard that she'd eventually got married and that she'd had a baby. I felt that, now she was safely ensconced on her wedding bed, she would drift out of my life altogether. But again I was wrong. One day the phone rang, and it was Ursula.

"Darling! It's *me*, Ursula!" she said.

"Good heavens!" I said, surprised. "Where have you been all these years?"

"Darling, I got *married*," she said. "I've had a baby."

"So I heard," I said. "Congratulations."

"Darling, I've been stuck down in the country for so long. I've got to come into Bournemouth today to do some shopping. I wondered whether we could meet?"

"Are you bringing your husband with you?" I asked cautiously.

"No, darling, I'm just coming on my own," she said.

"Well, in that case, by all means let us meet. I will buy you lunch. But first I'll meet you in the Cadena for coffee."

"Marvelous, darling. I'll be there at eleven o'clock," she said.

At eleven o'clock promptly she appeared through the doors of the Cadena café and I could see instantly that she was well on the way to expecting her second child. Apart from the protuberance of her stomach she had a glowing air about her, like rose petals in sunshine.

"Darling!" she screamed. "Darling! *Darling!*"

She flung her arms round me and gave me a prolonged kiss of the variety that is generally cut out of French films by the English censor. She made humming noises as she kissed, like a hive of sex-mad bees. She thrust her body against mine to extract the full flavor of the embrace and to show me that she really cared, really and truly. Several elderly ladies and what appeared to be a brigadier who had been preserved (like a plum in port) stared at us with fascinated repulsion. You could tell from their expressions that they expected me to rip her clothes off her and rape her there, on the sacred floor of the Cadena. I tore myself loose from her with an effort.

"I thought you were married," I said.

"I *am*, darling," she said. "Don't you think my kissing's improved?"

"Yes," I said. "Sit down and have some coffee."

"Can I have an ice cream?" she asked.

"All right," I said.

I ordered a coffee and an ice cream.

Ursula

"Well, I must say, you're looking blooming," I said.

"Do you think so?"

"I think you're looking wonderful. I see you're going to have another one."

She took a large mouthful of ice cream and spoke through it rather indistinctly.

"Children are absholutely marvelloush."

"So I believe," I said.

She swallowed her mouthful of ice cream and leant forward and tapped my wrist with her moist spoon to gain my full attention.

"Do you know what they say?" she inquired in her penetrating voice.

Every table in the restaurant suspended operations and waited expectantly. I felt I might as well be hung for a sheep as for a lamb.

"No," I said. "What do they say?"

"Why," she said, waving her spoon happily, "contraception is a woman's work."

We had coffee and then I took Ursula shopping, and later we went to lunch.

"Do you miss me, darling?" she inquired as she sipped at her wine.

"Of course I miss you," I said. "You were always one of my favorite girl friends."

"Isn't it a pity that one can't have boy friends *and* be married?" she said.

"Well, you can always try," I suggested.

"Oh, no, I couldn't do that," she said. "But you are sweet."

"Think nothing of it," I said.

"Anyway, I don't suppose you'd like me now," she said, wistfully. "I've reformed. I've become very dull."

"Do you think so?" I asked, thinking how vital and sweet she was still.

"Oh, yes," she said, looking at me solemnly with her great blue eyes. "I'm afraid I'm now what they call one of the petty beaujolais."

"Yes, but a vintage year," I said, raising my glass.

AFTERWORD

A message from the Durrell Wildlife Conservation Trust

The end of this book isn't the end of Gerald Durrell's story. The various experiences you have just read about gave impetus and inspiration to his lifetime crusade to preserve the rich diversity of animal life on this planet.

Although he died in 1995, the words of Gerald Durrell in this and his other books will continue to inspire people everywhere with love and respect for what he called "this magical world." His work goes on through the untiring efforts of the Durrell Wildlife Conservation Trust.

Over the years many readers of Gerald Durrell's books have been so motivated by his experiences and vision that they have wanted to continue the story for themselves by supporting the work of his Trust. We hope that you will feel the same way today because through his books and life, Gerald Durrell set us all a challenge. "Animals are the great voteless and voiceless majority," he wrote, "who can only survive with our help."

Please don't let your interest in conservation end when you turn this page. Write to us now and we'll tell you how you can be part of our crusade to save animals from extinction.

For further information, or to send a donation, write to

DURRELL WILDLIFE CONSERVATION TRUST
Les Augrès Manor
Jersey, Channel Islands, JE3 5BP UK
WWW.DURRELL.ORG

Eclipse Fever by Walter Abish
352 PAGES; *036-5; $15.95

The American Boy's Handy Book
by Daniel C. Beard
472 PAGES; 449-0; $12.95

The Book of Camp-Lore & Wood Craft
by Daniel C. Beard
288 PAGES; 352-6; $12.95

The American Girl's Handy Book
by Lina & Adelia Beard
496 PAGES; 666-3; $12.95

The Field & Forest Handy Book by Daniel C. Beard
448 PAGES; *165-5; $14.95

Borstal Boy by Brendan Behan
400 PAGES; 105-1; $16.95

La Bonne Table by Ludwig Bemelmans
448 PAGES; 808-9; $17.95

The Best of Beston by Henry Beston
208 PAGES; *104-3; $16.95

The Decline and Fall of Practically Everybody
by Will Cuppy
240 PAGES; 377-1; $15.95

How to Attract the Wombat by Will Cuppy
176 PAGES; *156-6; $14.95

How to Become Extinct by Will Cuppy
128 PAGES; *365-8; $14.95

How to Tell Your Friends from the Apes
by Will Cuppy
160 PAGES; *297-X; $15.95

Aubrey's Brief Lives by Oliver Lawson Dick (ed.)
408 PAGES; *063-2; $20.95

Beasts in My Belfry by Gerald Durrell
192 PAGES; *584-7; $16.95

Fauna and Family by Gerald Durrell
240 PAGES; *441-7; $15.95

Fillets of Plaice by Gerald Durrell
192 PAGES; *354-2; $15.95

Bear by Marian Engel
128 PAGES; 667-1; $13.95

The Kitchen Book & The Cook Book
by Nicolas Freeling
360 PAGES; 862-3; $17.95

Bright Stars, Dark Trees, Clear Water
by Wayne Grady (ed.)
336 PAGES; *019-5; $16.95

On Eagle Pond
by Donald Hall
272 PAGES; *560-X; $16.95

String Too Short to Be Saved
by Donald Hall
176 PAGES; *554-5; $14.95

Swimmer in the Secret Sea by William Kotzwinkle
96 PAGES; 356-9; $9.95

As I Walked Out One Midsummer Morning
by Laurie Lee
216 PAGES; *392-5; $15.95

Cider With Rosie by Laurie Lee
224 PAGES; 355-0; $15.95

A Moment of War by Laurie Lee
144 PAGES; *516-2; $15.95

Ring of Bright Water by Gavin Maxwell
344 PAGES; *400-X; $18.95

Giving Up the Gun by Noel Perrin
136 PAGES; 773-2; $12.95

Hamlet's Mill
by Giorgio de Santillana & Hertha von Dechend
576 PAGES; 215-3; $21.95

The Maine Reader
by Charles & Samuella Shain (eds.)
544 PAGES; *078-0; $20.95

Lark Rise to Candleford by Flora Thompson
936 PAGES; *363-1; $18.95

The Philosopher's Diet by Richard Watson
128 PAGES; *084-5; $14.95

The Philosopher's Demise by Richard Watson
128 PAGES; *227-9; $15.95

NB: *The* ISBN *prefix for titles with an asterisk is* 1-56792.
The prefix for all others is 0-87923.